Arist von Schlippe

The Carousel of Indignation and Outrage

Understanding the Nature of
Conflict Escalation and how to Limit it

VANDENHOECK & RUPRECHT

Bibliographic information published by the Deutsche Nationalbibliothek:
The Deutsche Nationalbibliothek lists this publication in the Deutsche Nationalbibliografie;
detailed bibliographic data available online: https://dnb.de.

© 2024 Vandenhoeck & Ruprecht, Robert-Bosch-Breite 10, D-37079 Göttingen,
an imprint of the Brill-Group (Koninklijke Brill BV, Leiden, Netherlands;
Brill USA Inc., Boston MA, USA; Brill Asia Pte Ltd, Singapore; Brill Deutschland GmbH,
Paderborn, Germany; Brill Österreich GmbH, Vienna, Austria)
Koninklijke Brill BV includes the imprints Brill, Brill Nijhoff, Brill Schöningh, Brill Fink,
Brill mentis, Brill Wageningen Academic, Vandenhoeck & Ruprecht, Böhlau and V&R unipress.

All rights reserved. No part of this work may be reproduced or utilized in any form or by
any means, electronic or mechanical, including photocopying, recording, or any information
storage and retrieval system, without prior written permission from the publisher.

Expanded and revised edition. The original edition *Das Karussell der Empörung* was published
in 2022 by the same publisher.

Cover image: svenkaiser2803/photocase.de
Proofreading: Annalena Greve

Typesetting: SchwabScantechnik, Göttingen
Printed and bound: ⊕ Hubert & Co, Ergolding
Printed in the EU

Vandenhoeck & Ruprecht Verlage | www.vandenhoeck-ruprecht-verlage.com

ISBN 978-3-525-40038-8

*Dedicated to my friend Jochen Schweitzer (†),
with heartfelt affection*

Foreword

When I was approached by Arist von Schlippe to write the foreword for this book, I could not have been more excited. Without revealing our age, Arist and I met a long time ago. I was just a fledging researcher and Arist was already a giant in the field. When I reached out to meet him for the first time, he could not have been nicer and more generous with his time. Based on this first meeting, we kept interacting and started working together on a few book chapters and journal-audience based research. At each step in our collaborations, I have always been impressed by the in-depth knowledge and wisdom that Arist exhibits, and I consider myself lucky to learn from him.

While most of Arist's work in published in German, we are fortunate that this book has been expertly translated and is now available for the English-speaking audience. As a conflict researcher, I believe that having this resource available will be useful to both conflict parties and counsellors alike.

When I think of carousels, I think of a circular motion: not really going anywhere, always ending up at the same point over and over again. The illustrator of the book had a similar notion; he shows a carousel with everyone yelling "Faster" or "I am the first" while turning in circles. I also associate the carousel with the notion of up and down movement. The carousel's animals go up and down, much as the ebb and flow of negative emotions that we experience.

However, on a positive note, I recall a particular scene from the movie, *Mary Poppins*, when Mary takes her wards and her friend Bert on a carousel ride. Indeed, Bert remarks that such a ride is very nice if one does not want to go anywhere. At this point, Mary, with the help of the carousel conductor, does her magic. The carousel figures break out of the circle and the entire group rides off to new, happy adventures.

The notion of a carousel serves Arist's conflict theme very well. Not only does he outline the ups and downs and the potential vicious cycle of conflict, but he also offers insights about how to break the circle and prevent conflict from escalating, even suggesting an exit. While the conflict parties may not all ride together into the sunset after reading this book, the profound knowledge that Arist has accumulated through decades as a consultant and professor will provide value for conflict parties and mediators alike. This book will raise awareness of the underlying issues of the conflict experience and the potential to get off the carousel ride once it has started.

I hope you will enjoy reading this book from the pre-eminent authority on conflict and its management in Germany as much as I did.

Prof. Dr. Franz W. Kellermanns (fkellerm@uncc.edu)
University of North Carolina – Charlotte (USA) and WHU – Otto Beisheim School of Management (USA)

Table of Contents

Foreword 7

Not a preface – but an "Instruction manual" for this book 13

PART ONE: DON'T BE AFRAID OF THEORY

1. **The shape of conflict** 19
   1.1 What is conflict, actually? 19
   1.2 Symmetry and complementarity 25

2. **Expectations, and the expectation of expectations** 32
   2.1 The improbability of order and understanding 32
   2.2 We are mutually inscrutable 34
   2.3 The concept of "expectations" 36
   2.4 The expectation of expectations 37
   2.5 A little side view 39
   2.6 Relationship disturbances and the metaperspective 40
   2.7 Interim summary 43

3. **Indignation and outrage: The engine of the carousel** 45
   3.1 Feelings in systemic therapy 45
   3.2 The little word "should" and the moral demand 48
   3.3 Indignation, outrage and justice 49
   3.4 Internal account management and justice 51
   3.5 Are outrage and indignation feelings? About affective-cognitive "Eigenwelten" 54
   3.6 A small exercise 57

4	How does communication know where it belongs?	58
	4.1 The context determines the meaning	58
	4.2 Context markers	60
	4.3 Polycontexturality	60
	4.4 What is a 'system' in social systems theory? An exploration through the lens of family business	62
	4.5 Conclusion	66
5	The experienced pressure of causality	68
	5.1 Causality – Just a pair of glasses?	68
	5.2 Deeply embedded epistemological patterns	70

PART TWO: RIDING THE CAROUSEL – LET'S GO!

6	Circularity and punctuation	75
	6.1 Who started it?	75
	6.2 The paradox of simplification	78
7	Disappointed expectations	80
	7.1 The power of expectations	80
	7.2 Implicit promises: Psychological contracts	83
	7.3 Disappointed expectations and the "deep story"	85
	7.4 The implicit relationship contract in couples	87
8	Hit where it hurts: Experience and self-esteem	89
9	The one-sided view: Perception in conflict	96
	9.1 The one-sided view (Part 1): Person-related attribution and motive attribution	97
	9.2 The one-sided view (Part 2): Perceptual distortions	99
	The fundamental attribution error	99
	The hostile perception error	100
	9.3 The one-sided view (Part 3): Protecting rigid viewpoints and the confirmation bias	103
	9.4 Groupthink: The equalisation of communication	104
	9.5 Interim summary	105
10	Stupid, sick or evil: Demonisation	106

11 Watch out: Dangerous thoughts ... 111
11.1 The belief in the myth of power ... 113
11.2 Thinking in binary categories ... 115
11.3 Our superiority and the otherness of others ... 116
11.4 Basic distrust, conspiracies and secrecy ... 118
11.5 The need for an immediate response ... 119
11.6 Sunk costs ... 119

12 Faster and faster: High-speed communication ... 121

13 The memory of social systems: The transgenerational transmission of conflict ... 126

14 We've created a monster: The conflict as a parasitic social system ... 131
14.1 The conflict system ... 131
14.2 Demoralisation ... 134

15 Not one step further: The horsemen of the apocalypse and the abyss ... 136
15.1 The nine stages of escalation ... 136
15.2 The horsemen of the apocalypse ... 140

PART THREE: PATHWAYS THROUGH CONFLICT – THE POSSIBLE EXIT

16 The rehabilitation of outrage and indignation ... 149

17 Who reigns when war reigns? Thoughts on the 'management' of conflicts ... 152

18 "Consciousness raising", becoming aware of automatic mechanisms and self-work ... 155
18.1 The art of the unexpected response ... 156
18.2 "The First-Aid break" ... 160
18.3 "Neither too many nor too few words!" ... 161
18.4 Resisting the temptation to demonise ... 162
18.5 Mind your language! ... 163
18.6 Symbolic gestures and good moments ... 164
18.7 Regrets ... 166

19 Positions and interests: "Why is this important to you?" ... 168

20 The balcony perspective and the blind spot 170
  20.1 Self-observation 170
  20.2 The carousel of expectations 171
  20.3 The reflecting team 172
  20.4 Reflective positions 174

21 The "third element" 176
  21.1 A person or principle as "the third party" 176
  21.2 The importance of a grand gesture 179

PART FOUR: TEN RECOMMENDATIONS FOR DEALING WITH CONFLICTS

References 184

Not a preface – but an "Instruction manual" for this book

The task of understanding conflicts and their dynamics and finding ways to address them has occupied me increasingly in recent decades. I have already written about this subject in various places, often with reference to entrepreneurial families: my specialist field as a family therapist in recent years. This book will summarise much of the content of these scattered publications under the metaphor of the carousel – a symbol for the circular organisation of processes within conflict systems. It would take too long to list the many colleagues from whom I have learned, with whom I have collaborated and with whom I have written texts but, in this regard, I must highlight my friend and colleague Haim Omer from Tel Aviv. His thoughts on helping families in highly escalated conflict situations to escape the dilemma between compliance or escalation by pursuing non-violent perseverance have had a profound impact on me.

Regarding the somewhat ambitious intention of this book: I would like to reach you, as a reader, first and foremost personally, whether you are yourself caught in an escalating conflict, whether you feel helpless observing those close to you in conflict, or whether you have to deal with conflictual relationships – at whatever level – in a professional capacity, as a supervisor or consultant. I would be pleased if you would reflect as often as possible while reading the book and ask yourself what the words written mean in your everyday life, your family relationships, and your practical environment. I would be happy if you become curious to notice where the text changes your perspective – be it on everyday events or conflict issues.

Occasionally, I will suggest transferring one thing or another into your own "conflict notebook"; the illustration in the margin here highlights these opportunities. At the same time, I am interested in making suggestions about dealing with conflict, whether it be about the manner in which we manoeuvre our own "conflict boat" through the rapids of escalation or how, as a practically active person, to support others in this endeavor. Finally, I would also like to contribute to the academic debate on the topic and show that the ideas of systems theory can be extremely helpful in understanding conflicts. This whole project aims to strike a balance – avoiding frightening off lay people and practitioners while not slipping under the radar in the academic field. I welcome your feedback. For their critical comments and suggestions during the writing of the book, I sincerely thank my wife, Rita, my esteemed colleagues Anita von Hertel, Franziska von Kummer, Lina Nagel, Barbara Ollefs and Susanne Quistorp, and my invaluable friend and colleague Jürgen Kriz. A big thank-you goes to my daughter Anna Greve, she gave me brilliant, critical and very precise remarks in working on the translation. Without her support, I might have despaired at the task.

But now, let us move on to the instruction manual: the book has three major parts, which can be read in sequence or independently of one another.

The first part is entitled "Don't be afraid of theory". Hmm, I wonder whether that will work. Well, I have tried to write as simply and understandably as possible and to clearly mark the occasional deeper dives, so that anyone who does not yet dare to venture into deeper waters can safely skip those parts (e. g. Chapter 4, especially 4.4), or read them just two pages at a time after dinner (we're in the "instruction manual" here, after all). You could also skip the first part altogether or read only the chapter on indignation (even just from 3.2), which lays the foundations for understanding the engine of the carousel.

Or you could turn straight to the second major part and start riding the carousel. Here, I describe the many well-studied processes of social and conflict psychology, which strongly influence our thinking, perceiving, and remembering in conflictual communication contexts. I have always been interested in these mechanisms that we humans inherited from our ancestors from time immemorial. There is no need to follow the sequence of the chapters here – their content often overlaps and so you can jump to whichever heading attracts you – like riding a carousel, you can sit on one horse or another, they all go in the same direction. The second particular focus of the book is also connected with this part. My intention is to raise awareness of how much we are in danger of simply letting these inherited mechanisms take over when we are in conflict situations, without thinking or reflecting on what we are doing. They evolved long ago to help us react quickly in simple or only moderately complex environments where the alternatives were often life or death. That is why they disguise themselves so skilfully: we think we are acting rationally and are in possession of all our senses, but we are actually hypnotised by what is happening and, under the spell of this "conflict-hypnosis", our actions lead to escalation. These mechanisms are so dangerous, on small and large scales. If we are not aware of them, they can lead us like sleepwalkers into small and also into large wars (impressively described in Clark, 2013, regarding the First World War; let us hope that we have learnt something from that time but I am not entirely sure).

Why is conscious awareness of these processes so important to me? I have always been convinced by the words of the British-American anthropologist Gregory Bateson on the premises of human actions: "In a word, your perceptual machinery, the way you perceive, is governed by a system of presuppositions that I call your epistemology: a whole philosophy deep inside your mind but beyond your consciousness" (Bateson & Bateson, 2005, p. 136[1], see also Chapter 18 in this book). One of Bateson's main concerns was raising awareness of the implicit philosophy governing people's actions, knowing that this can only ever be partially possible because "[...] we are not by any means the captains of our souls" (Bateson, 1972, p. 444).

If you so wish, you can also read the book back to front, beginning with the practical outlook in the third part. However, I deliberately did not set out to write a "conflict guidebook" or practical handbook, and I certainly did not want to reinvent the various intervention methods. There are many good books available with so-called toolboxes for this purpose and we also have a broad knowledge of practical methods of conflict resolution and mediation. Methodologically, I have little to add to these and would rather provide you with *thinking tools*. In this last part, therefore, I have outlined basic features of systemic conflict work that are easy to follow and can be useful in conflict resolution. In my first (German) book on conflict (von Schlippe, 2014c), I described three perspectives from which to constructively influence conflict events – as an affected party, an observer or a professional. Perhaps the third part of this book will offer some suggestions as well, without trying to pretend that any of these steps are easily feasible, instant, or complete solutions. I tend to be rather cautious about the chances of success when working with people in highly escalated conflicts. It is preferable not to expect Hollywood-style reconciliations ("Forgive me!"), but rather to appreciate the many small steps that sometimes improve the situation just a little. I simply mean by this that we should not set the bar too high. But it is certainly never in vain to work on one's own consciousness when "under the influence" of a conflict.

---

1   Some citations originally in English were translated back from the German by myself. I was unable to find all the original titles that I had used in German versions of books that had come out in English first. In these cases, the citation may differ from the original, and page numbers then refer to the German edition. I have listed the German source first in the reference list, and the English version second. If the English translation of an original German text is placed first in the reference list, then the citation is taken from the translation, and the page numbers refer to the English source.

PART ONE: DON'T BE AFRAID OF THEORY

In this part, I intend to make basic suggestions that can offer an understanding of conflicts and their dynamics, as mentioned, from the perspective of those personally affected as well as from a professional point of view. Precisely because many people respond to the word "theory" with a mixture of respect, fear and/or disinterest, I aim to approach the subject in such a way that the considerations presented can be translated directly and practically into private and professional day-to-day life. If a reader at least occasionally recognises themselves in the descriptions, my aim has been achieved.

My wish to promote an understanding of conflict lies at the heart of this book. It is not so much about providing a list of methods and tools for resolving conflicts (with alluring but sometimes also misleading promises of fast results). Rather, my focus is on understanding. Those who understand the dynamics of conflicts may also understand themselves better. The ability to understand oneself and others is possibly the best defence against the destructive escalation of conflict dynamics. Jay Forrester is credited with saying "The human mind is not suited to understanding human social systems" (quoted in Riedl, 1981, p. 89). But this should not mean, in my view, that we should not at least try.

1 The shape of conflict

> "We do not live in the sort of universe in which simple lineal control is possible. Life is not like that ... We are by no means the captains of our souls" (Bateson, 1972, p. 444).

1.1 What is conflict, actually?

Conflict is part of everyday human life. It is often seen negatively but can act as an engine of change in many different social situations. It forces us to adopt a clear position and stand up for our own beliefs and perspectives. In many conflict situations, negotiation and debate lead to long-term, sustainable results. Family life, in particular, is an important playing field for learning conflict resolution skills. In organisations, too, cognitive, factual conflicts about "tasks" (*what is* to be done) and "processes" (*how* is it to be done) are by no means considered problematic, because they bring the potential for positive outcomes and stimulate creativity and innovation (for a broad overview see Jehn, 2014; see also Jehn, 1997; Kellermanns & Eddleston, 2007; Rispens, 2014). It is difficult to imagine how a company could develop and grow without these conflicts.

However, conflict should not be trivialised. Once a conflict has arisen, the dynamics can easily take on a life of their own: disputes on a factual level can quickly shift from being focused on "tasks" and "processes" to becoming issues about "relationships". It is this type of conflict that is responsible for the negative image of conflict. Emotions run ever higher, and the behavior of the actors becomes ever more irrational (at least from an outside perspective), even though those involved usually believe that they have everything under control. In reality, they have long since ceased to be "captains of their souls" and are unwittingly caught in a vicious circle (as the quote from Bateson that precedes this chapter suggests). Insults, slights and even physical attacks often cause lasting damage to the relationships between them, whether the differences are openly heated or covertly icy (Glasl, 2002; 2014a, 2014b). The damage to relationships is often significant: social systems can break apart, people leave their jobs, or get divorced, and much more.

It is this type of escalating conflict that is the primary concern of this book. Therefore, its focus will be on understanding and managing the destructive side of conflicts. It does not necessarily follow, as mentioned above, that conflicts should be seen as inherently negative. On the contrary, the better we know and understand the dynamics which can take over an important factual dispute, the more constructively solutions can be found. "The difficulty in harnessing the positive, constructive potential of conflict stems from the fact that the negative, destructive potential is so great. As a result, the opportunity inherent in conflict is often not exploited in order to avoid the risk involved" (Simon, 2012, p. 36).[2] Therefore, we must consciously address the issues in any conflict; a mere "Enough now, let's all get on and shake hands!" is not sufficient. The task is to raise consciousness in the sense of developing a sensitivity to the development and maintenance of conflict dynamics (Harvey & Evans, 1994) or, to paraphrase the words of my colleague and friend Jochen Schweitzer: most conflicts are the result of an unintentional joint effort, and an intentional joint effort is required for their resolution or alleviation.[3]

Enough of the preface, let us now jump to the moment when it becomes clear that "We have a conflict!" What do we actually "have"? A conflict is not (as Figure 1 suggests) an object, one that can be measured. Although it is sometimes said of a conflict that it is large, heavy or light, no one has ever measured it in metres or kilograms (as far as I know). Interestingly, we also say *"we* have".[4] Somehow, two or more people jointly have this "it". Sometimes the other person answers that they see "it" differently: "No, we don't have a conflict, it's just a difference of opinion!" Aha, so there are obviously degrees of conflict.

However, when it comes to a "real conflict" (hmm, what is that again?), the last thing both parties agree on is that they disagree. Often there is no explicit starting point: we slip into it, one word leads to another and – out of nowhere – the conflict is there. "No, no," one of the parties tells the consultant, "It's not out of nowhere. If you knew what she had done!" – "Wait a minute," says the other, "Please, don't believe a word he says, that's exactly the problem – he's messing everything up! It was he who started it, and I'll tell you the story. It was like this ..." – "Stop!" he[5] interrupts again, "That's just it, she just doesn't see her part in this! This will destroy our relationship if it goes on. I ask you – seriously, do we have to put up with this?"

---

2   Citations from original German sources were translated by myself.
3   He applies this more generally to psychosocial problems, but that is what conflicts are.
4   Of course, a person can also be in conflict with themself but, even then, there are two opposing sides. This book is exclusively about social conflicts.
5   From time to time, I will use gender designations in an alternating manner; I do not like "gendering" throughout, even though I fully share the underlying concern not to exclude anyone linguistically. However, I regard asterisks, underscores and other signs as problematic, ideologically motivated interventions in language, which I do not want to adopt. The theme of different and diverse genders should certainly be recognisable throughout the book as food for thought, without the language having to contort itself too much.

What is conflict, actually?

Figure 1: A "real" conflict (drawing and copyright: Björn von Schlippe)

So, have we made some progress now on what conflict is? Yes, a little: it is not a "thing", but a "some-thing" of some intensity (and more than just a difference of opinion) which takes place between two or more people. It takes the form of a chain of contradictions – or at least the tendency is to negate rather than concur: a pattern has emerged. In this sense, conflicts are everyday occurrences, usually resolved as quickly as they arise. Of interest to us are those that do not simply vanish. But only something that is there can disappear. In what way is a conflict "there"? You cannot see it; you may hear two people shouting at each other or sarcastically disparaging one another; you may see closed faces, frowns, bruises or worse, but you cannot see the conflict itself in the way that you see a thing. We experience it ourselves if we were involved; we can feel it in the atmosphere as an observer and name it accordingly ("You could cut the atmosphere with a knife here!") or describe it as a dynamic pattern, perhaps even distinguishing between different stages of escalation (Glasl, 2002, 2014b; see also Chapter 15). In whichever case, it is clear that two (or more) people have constructed a strange (and at the same time familiar) form of communication from which they cannot easily exit.

The form of the conflict seems to be characterised by constant contradiction; a permanent "no" punctuates communication between the parties, whether individuals or groups (Bonacker and Imbusch, 2004, p. 196). At the same time, conflict (here we are talking of "relationship conflict" in which facts play a decreasing role) also seems to be characterised by a primarily one-directional process: the level of contradiction in the communication tends to intensify, moving from factual differences to the devaluation of – and direct attacks on – the other. It becomes less and less about the matter at hand because the self-esteem of the person concerned is now being attacked: the ego is "under siege" (Pfab, 2020, p. 2). Generalised statements starting with "always" or "never" are made and may even lead to physical aggression. The communication continues – as it does in any other communication system – but room for manoeuvre is lost. Few options remain, and the common denominator of those that do is to communicate a 'no' to the other, i.e. to reject offers of communication. Can we therefore say that 'conflict is a dynamic of an intensifying mutual negation?'

Yes, there is something to that. As already mentioned, you cannot have a conflict alone. Let us say that one person wants to holiday by the sea, the other in the mountains (and they don't know that in Asturias in the North of Spain they can have both together!). As long as both keep this desire to themselves, there is no conflict. Only when these wishes are communicated is there a chance that a conflict system will form. This requires a contradiction: "Mountains?" – "No, sea!" Still, that alone is not a conflict, something else is needed: the communicated contradiction must in turn be answered with another contradiction (Luhmann, 1995, 1996). Conflict needs a "double negation": the 'no' is again negated (Simon, 2012). The word "dynamics" already indicates that this contradiction is not solely one sided: this is a *system of* contradicting each other. A conflict is a certain form of communication sequence: a communication is answered with a negation, and this is followed again by a negation. This kind of mirror-image reaction to each other is called *"symmetrical"*: formally, each side responds in the same way, or with more of the same, thus creating an escalation,[6] while conceding is called *"complementary"* (Bateson, 1972; Watzlawick, Beavin, and Jackson, 1967; more on this later in the chapter).

Only when a chain of such symmetrically related negations is recognisable do we "have" a conflict: "I would like to go on holiday to the sea this year!" – "Oh no, we've been there so often. I'd like to go to the mountains!" We already know that this alone is not enough – it is as if the match is lit, but that alone

---

6 In this sense, the small exercise in escalation, which can be carried out well in a seminar, is also symmetrical in form: the participants face each other in pairs and begin a "Yes!"-"No!" spiral, which usually increases quickly in volume. "No!" and "Yes" are complementary words, but here they negate each other as contradiction from the form. A complementary answer to the yes or the no would be for example: "All right!" or "Agreed!"

does not start a fire; even if the paper is already burning, it is easily put out. The possibility of a complementary exit is still within reach: "Well, then, we'll just do it the way you want!" or "How about a city trip this time?" But once the kindling catches fire, the thicker logs also have a chance. From here, it is still a long way to a forest fire, but it always starts like this, with the "match of the first contradiction", the subsequent negation of the negation and thereafter its symmetrical negation: "But I want to go to the sea!" – "Oh, not again – you always want your own way!" (aha, let's also remember this: a conflict often has a longer history. Old grudges are dragged into it: it's not just about the holiday destination, but about the fact that, from the perspective of one person, it's always the other who gets their own way and this frustrates them) – "You do too, you're such a hypocrite!" – "I'll tell you one thing: I'm definitely not going to the sea with you this year, you can be sure of that!" – "Okay, if you're going to be like that, then I'll go on my own!" – "There's no need to be so aggressive!" – "I'm not being aggressive!" Positions are built up that are difficult to abandon (more to that in Chapter 19). We can imagine how the conversation continues.

Sooner or later, we get into dangerous waters: the positions harden. With every interaction, every communication that follows on from another in a conflictual – negating and defensive – manner, the conflict takes on a life of its own. The emerging conflict system takes over and, without noticing it, the parties relinquish their ability to control the situation and begin following the conflict system that they – and this is the exciting thing about these self-organising dynamics – have created themselves. As observers, we can see how, again and again, both parties try to control the dynamics, to de-escalate the conflict: "Come on, let's talk reasonably with each other!" – but the pattern cannot be broken so easily, as we quickly recognise from the other's response: "Sure, fine with me! Then stop talking all that nonsense! It's not up to me, anyway!" and the conflict system is back on track.[7] Usually, we do not realise which internal psychological

---

7   This is masterfully captured in the play *The God of Carnage* by Yasmina Reza, also made into a film: all four characters (two couples) are benevolent and focused on a solution. They meet to talk about a quarrel between their respective sons, one of whom has knocked out the other's front teeth with a stick. Now the letter to the insurance company has to be formulated. They try hard to keep the conflict under control ("We can talk about it like adults!" or "Would you like another sip of tea?") but a conflict system quickly develops between them. It is presented as a force of its own, which, shortly before a possibly constructive end to a scene, repeatedly causes one of the four to make an escalating comment such as "But one *must* say that what your son did to ours was violence!" – And then it continues, the others react indignantly: "Well, we'll have to discuss that now, it won't do!" This, after already having said good-bye ... they sit down again and the conflict pattern continues. The conversation ends in disaster while, in the final scene, the two boys who had quarrelled are already playing peacefully with each other again.

processes lead us to choose the 'one and only reality' that we take as 'truth'. Kriz emphasises "that we often lack awareness of the power of interpersonal dynamics and that our 'conscious' explanation of only reacting to the other person is neither correct nor helpful" (Kriz, 2017b, p. 192 f.). These mechanisms contribute significantly to the fact that the conflict patterns are so resistant to change. We will discuss this in detail in the later chapters of this book.

Although we are still in the introduction, I would like to give in to the temptation to refer to a diagram which describes the relationship between the single *elements* (the small lower squares in Figure 2) and the *system* (the larger upper rectangle). More precisely, it illustrates how a "field" or even a system is created from individual small actions. The picture helped me to understand the phenomenon of the self-organisation of communication systems in general and of conflict systems in particular: two parties (individuals or groups) generate their own communication system from their interactions (sometimes we might jokingly say in this context, "Uh oh – it looks like you've 'created a monster'!" about the pattern they have generated in the course of their communication history, see Chapter 14). Once this "monster" has emerged – and this is the interesting thing – it begins to control the interactions, and the options available to the participants become increasingly limited. This leads Luhmann to speak of a "highly integrated social system" in which communication options are ever more restricted (Luhmann, 1996, p. 479).

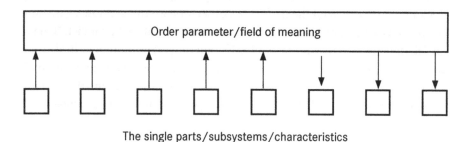

Figure 2: Pattern formation as a circular process (Kriz, 2009, p. 637).

The small squares represent the single interactions: all the example sentences given previously. The large rectangle above has been created by these interactions (arrows go first from the bottom to the top) and has thus become an 'order parameter' (Haken, 1992). Although only the initial interactions formed the ordering pattern or field of meaning, after some time this pattern in turn determines further interactions (arrows from top to bottom). Imagine a melody which is initially formed from single tones but once the melody is established it determines which tones fit and which do not. The melody now "governs" the tones; a sentence "governs" the words and, once a conflict has arisen, it "governs" or reigns subsequent interactions (see chapter 17); of course, the process is much more complex than with melodies. Kriz cites a simple, particularly illustrative example: in the applause after a concert, we have all experienced how all of a sudden, out of nowhere, hundreds of unconnected clapping motions transform into a rhythmic pattern. Everyone claps to the same rhythm and, although the rhythm had emerged from the clapping movements, it now in turn controls the clapping movements. The pattern emerges spontaneously and rapidly dissolves again (Kriz, 2017b, p. 107).

We see similar self-organising phenomena in other situations, for example, at the start of a weekend seminar you look for your seat. After the break, you sit there again, but after lunch, someone else is sitting there. You are irritated: "Hey, this is 'my' seat!" How the situation unfolds from there may depend on whether the seminar in question is about group-dynamics, team building or business ... The important point is that patterns emerge from manners of behaving and communicating. These, in turn, influence those same behaviours and communications. This is less problematic with simple, fleeting patterns in interaction systems, but can become quite dramatic when two parties communicate together in a conflict system.

1.2 Symmetry and complementarity

Through their interactions, the actors have now created a *field,* a circular self-reinforcing conflict system that leads into a dynamic of increasing escalation.[8] We can imagine how it will continue if there are no brakes: after all, one of them has already threatened to go to the sea alone, if necessary, and they seem unlikely to send each other friendly postcards from their separate holidays. Thus, we suspect that the separate holidays will perhaps lead to a more permanent separation and the end of the relationship (love had already disappeared some time ago). This is then one possible way for a conflict to end – with the

---

[8] As a counsellor, when dealing with circular dynamics it is advisable to resist being drawn into believing the claims of any one particular side about what the start point of a "cycle" may have been ("She started it!" – "No, he did!"). "In principle, if you want to explain or understand anything in human behavior, you are always dealing with total circuits, completed circuits" (Bateson, 1972, p. 465; see also Nagel, 2021). We come back to this topic in Chapter 6.1.

breakup of the social system. Gregory Bateson coined the somewhat impenetrable term "schismogenesis" for this phenomenon, i.e. the emergence of division, of separation (Bateson, 1972, p. 67).

As previously mentioned, Bateson distinguished between two forms of communicative reaction to the statement or position of another – symmetrical and complementary. In his ethnological research, conducted together with Margaret Mead, on the Iatmul, a South Sea people, he found that the Iatmul had developed complex rules to regulate the escalation of symmetry. Bateson described as "symmetrical" any communication in which "like is answered with like", such as the aforementioned negation spiral. In *symmetry*, the logic of sameness prevails: like is repaid with like, with the built-in dynamics of increase and aggravation, and the danger of explosion if no one applies the brakes. In the second pattern that he identified, *complementarity*, the reaction is to de-escalate ("All right I give in!"). This, too, can potentially lead to division: it may involve collecting "credits" to be redeemed at some point: "That's enough, I'm always supposed to give in, you never do, that's it now!" A complementary dynamic is quieter and less conspicuous, but it can also escalate, in that as one party demands more and more, the other gives more and more, until one side collapses,[9] or the dynamics suddenly turn into high symmetry when the yielding party has finally had enough (we talk here also of hot and cold conflict dynamics, see Glasl, 2002, 2014a, 2014b). Therefore, faced with significant one-sided compliance, we should be on our guard (as is well-known, the smarter one gives in until he is the dumber one).

Bateson sees symmetry and complementarity as the two possible forms that an interaction can take. We can observe the complex interplay of symmetrical and complementary interactions in everyday life. Most of the time, both parties intuitively "play" the keyboard of symmetry and complementarity in such a way that destructive escalation is prevented. Each side gives in a little, then holds their position and then gives in again but the risk is always present that this process of mutual demanding and giving-in will be derailed. One-sidedness may become a problem here: that is when a system becomes stuck on predominantly symmetrical or permanently complementary interactions. Fortunately, humans are usually able to limit potential escalations. We learn to negotiate, to argue, to get along, to compromise ("Okay, one more trip to the sea this year,

---

9   Such complementary patterns of "collusion" are seen in couple dynamics, where the partners fill a need in the other over a long period (for example, when one enjoys being taken care of and the other feels comfortable in the role as "the strong one" who gives). Such dynamics can turn into depressive patterns: the weak one becomes weaker and weaker – "If I didn't have you!" – while the other reaches their limits of giving (Willi, 1982).

but next year …"). Without symmetry, there would be no change, we might be frozen in apparent "deadly politeness"[10] (Schulz von Thun, 2014), and it would be difficult to come to a mutually negotiated decision – mountains versus sea – without one of the parties keeping a "credit score". It is important to acknowledge this positive function of conflict, which fulfils a stabilising function in a social system. A system that is based only on one-sided concessions is very vulnerable if a conflict arises and its members have never learnt how to cope with communicated contradictions, therefore getting very upset when the "credit score" is presented by the one who is ready to "cash in their chips". Thus, conflict fulfils an "alarm function" (Luhmann, 1995), indicating that the conditions of the relationship need to be re-negotiated.

However, the reverse is also true: without complementarity, without moving towards each other (made sometimes by one, sometimes the other), there would be no agreement. When the conflict system gets stuck in one mode, the members of the social system are at risk – quieter and more depressed in rigid complementarity, louder and more heated in the escalating symmetry of a power struggle. A dynamic of unlimited escalation can become destructive and can lead people to murder and manslaughter; its dynamics can lead to wars (Simon, 2001). Therefore, Luhmann also speaks of 'parasitic social systems' (more on this later). This metaphor indicates that the conflict system "tends to draw the host system into conflict to the extent that all attention and all resources are claimed for the conflict" (Luhmann, 1995, p. 390).

It is, therefore, important to learn to understand conflict dynamics in order "to love them and limit them" (Eidenschink, 2023). One of the most important steps in conflict counselling, in my opinion, is that both parties realise that the primary goal is to limit escalation. This can succeed if both can see the jointly generated conflict system (the "monster" they have "created") as the true challenge.[11] This book was written not least for that reason: anyone who knows about the mechanisms involved in conflict systems; about the deeply ingrained reaction patterns that originate from primaeval times when we had to fight for survival every day, can develop an awareness of these mechanisms within themselves and so learn how to resist them, at least partially, instead of simply following them

---

10 This relates to a play on words in German: "Fried-Höflichkeit" combines the words "cemetery" (Friedhof) and "politeness" (Höflichkeit): too often politely giving in may be the death of a relationship.
11 A connection to the systemic intervention of externalisation can easily be recognised here (von Schlippe & Schweitzer, 2015; see also 2012, p. 270 ff.).

Figure 3: The carousel of indignation and outrage (drawing and copyright: Björn von Schlippe)

unreflectively. Conflict work thus also means working on the epistemology of the persons involved.[12]

In previous texts, I have compared conflict dynamics to a journey with a succession of stops along the way (see, for example, von Schlippe, 2019a). Here, the metaphor of the carousel will be taken as a starting point: entering a conflict system is like getting on a carousel. If you do not realise that you are on such a roundabout, you think that you have everything under control; that you alone are assessing the situation correctly and steering your (toy) fire engine in the right direction (see Figure 3). But "life is not like that", to refer to the Bateson quote at the beginning of the text. Often, we are only holding the toy steering wheel of a carousel car in our hands; the real steering is coming from somewhere else entirely. The carousel turns according to its own logic, and part of the problem is that those riding on it are under the illusion that they have the

---

12 I do not wish to discuss the differences between epistemology, constructivism, or social constructionism any further in this context; that has been done extensively elsewhere (cf. Bateson, 1972; Maturana & Varela, 1987). In essence, the point is that what people experience as "reality" is not a passive reflection of the reality that happens "out there" but "the result of an active cognition" (von Ameln, 2004, p. 3).

dynamics under control. Usually, there are two or more people on the carousel, chasing one another in the expectation of being able to overtake each other. An astute observation by Fritz B. Simon states that a conflict continues as long as each of the participants still has some hope of defeating the other. It could also be the other way around: one person may be sitting on the carousel and constantly looking behind for fear of being overtaken by the other. Then you fight not to lose, which sometimes exacerbates the dynamics even more. In both cases, these are agonising carousel games. In this sense, this book is an invitation to a carousel ride, with the goal of getting to know the carousel and the chances to get it stopped. At each stop, we can jump off – daring to take a step into something new and different – or we can continue the roundabout and allow ourselves to be taken over by the dynamics of the conflict.

The essence of the previous musings could be distilled to the quintessential idea that conflicts are the social phenomena of the "in-between": the processes formed of the interactions and feelings that take place in between two or more people. These conflicts tend to become autonomous as conflict systems, which increasingly determine the dynamics of the interaction. It is the job of conflict counselling to manage this in-between, this "monster" of our own creation. The great advantage of a systems-theoretical view of conflict is that it helps us to shift away from the idea that the conflict lies somewhere "inside" a person, that it derives from their mistakes and that it lies in their power to stop it (opinions on who should be the one to change usually vary in any case). Social systems theory assumes that a social system consists not of people but of the ways in which one communication connects to another (Luhmann, 1995; 2013). This is true for any communication system (more on this in Section 4.4), not just conflicts. Patterns emerge, but they usually allow enough room for multiple different connections: symmetric or complementary. But once a conflict is established, the variety of reactions is restricted and therefore the number of possible connections is drastically reduced: "Conflicts ...are *highly integrated social systems* because there is a tendency to bring all action into the context of an opposition within the perspective of opposition ... The system attains too great an interdependence: one word leads to another; every activity must and can be answered by another one" (Luhmann, 1995, p. 390, italicisation: AvS). As long as people move within the system logic of the conflict, they can only escalate the conflict further. As a consultant, I sometimes see first-hand how desperately the actors try to steer a system that has developed – and how they repeatedly experience that communication cannot be steered unilaterally, indeed that even attempts at clarification, mediation or reconciliation often fail, as illustrated in the following cartoon (Figure 4).

Figure 4: Madness (Drawing and copyright: Björn von Schlippe)

Escalations can also arise as "unintended consequences of action" (Merton, cited in Ortmann, 2003, p. 13) from unsuccessful attempts to resolve a conflict. The advantage of this understanding of (social) conflicts as a process independent of the individual parties involved is that it is not essential to look at specific occasions or conflict contents or to analyse the possible motives of the respective adversaries. This may help in trying to understand the pattern without becoming too distracted by the specific issues. It is the self-organised and continued negation of the negation that constitutes the conflict; with its interruption or termination, the conflict ends. (Caution, this sounds simpler than it is!)[13]

With these considerations in mind, let us conclude this section by looking at three different definitions from the social systems literature:

- "[...] we will therefore speak of conflict when a communication is contradicted, or when a contradiction is communicated. A conflict is the operative autonomisation of a contradiction through communication. Thus, a conflict exists when expectations are communicated and the nonacceptance of the communication is communicated in return" (Luhmann, 1995, p. 388).

---

13 This is encapsulated neatly in the following saying: In theory, the difference between theory and practice is much smaller than it is in practice ... Nevertheless – as this chapter hopes – theory can also provide helpful impulses for practice.

- "Conflict is to be defined as a communication process (= social process) or a thinking and feeling process (= psychological process) in which a position (e.g. a wish, an instruction to act, an option or effect, a point of view, an evaluation, etc.) is *negated* and this negation is *negated* in turn [...] This type of "meaning system",[14] which is characterised by a process of the continued negation of negations should be called a conflict. Its result is a state of undecidability. It lasts as long as the conflict lasts" (Simon, 2012, p. 11, italics in the original).
- "Social conflicts, generally speaking, consist of incompatible expectations on the part of at least two parties. This incompatibility must be perceived as such by the parties and can be reflected, for example, in conflicting interests or differing views" (Bonacker & Imbusch, 2004, p. 196).

These definitions reflect well what has been said so far. They describe how a chain of interaction events develops into a conflict system through a process of mutual contradiction, which – once it has arisen – continues in a self-organised way and intensifies in the process. This aspect is least recognisable in the third definition, which in my opinion is a little short-sighted (clashes of interests or different views are not automatically conflicts). On the other hand, a concept appears which is only briefly touched upon in Luhmann's first definition, although it plays a major role in the theory of social systems: that of expectations. The role that these play as a driver of the conflict of dynamics will be discussed in the following chapter.

---

14 Social systems theory sees social and psychological systems as systems based on meaning/significance/sense.

2 Expectations, and the expectation of expectations

2.1 The improbability of order and understanding

> "Social order, the unsubstantial cohesion of society, is always disturbed. Rules, oddly enough, always include their own transgression." (Ortmann, 2003, p. 11)

One question that concerns sociology in general, and systems theory in particular, is that of what creates social order. A prominent figure who pursued this question from a sociological perspective was the German social theorist Niklas Luhmann (1927–1998). His goal was to question self-evident aspects of our everyday life that we generally simply accept unquestioningly, that is "to seek theories that can succeed in explaining the normal as improbable" (Luhmann, 1995, p. 114). For example, Luhmann asks how, given the improbability of communication, we succeed in communicating at all (Luhmann, 1981). How is it possible to create shared meaning through sounds and signs? How does the self-organisation of our social life actually occur? The fact that people manage to communicate is already an enormous achievement: "At the zero point of evolution, it is, first of all, improbable that ego understands what alter[15] means – given that their bodies and minds are separate and individual" (Luhmann, 1995, p. 158).

Thus, he highlights three improbabilities:
a) It is "unlikely that one will even understand what the other means".
b) is "unlikely that a communication will reach more people than are present in a specific situation" and
c) success is unlikely, because despite understanding and achieving, there is no guarantee that the communication "will also be accepted" (Grizelj, 2012, p. 99; Luhmann, 1995, p. 157 ff.).

---

15 The words ego and alter are used by Luhmann to designate "the one" and "the other."

Although this book is on a different level from social theory and we will mainly address small social structures and the psychological issues that occur in the context of closer social relations, the initial problem is the same: you never can be sure about what will happen in social interactions. In any contact between two people there are multiple possible outcomes. This is called the problem of "contingency";[16] it is about the fact of the inscrutable and unpredictable nature of the other. One of the basic demands of human life however, indeed of life in general, is to find a way through situations that are, at least initially, completely inscrutable – unpredictability is difficult to endure. It is known, for example, that even the simplest living beings scan their environment for order structures from the very beginning and are sensitive to changes (such as the day-night rhythm) (Kriz, 2017b, p. 70 f.). If they are to survive, they must orient themselves in the order of the world. This is equally true of a child's development; in an infinite number of learning steps, it orients itself in the living world into which it was born (Stern, 2016). In contrast to single-celled organisms, the main task here, in addition to learning daily routines, the weather, meals, etc., is to first become familiar with the social structures in which everyday life takes place, and then to begin to actively shape them. This is the enormous achievement of the human species over the course of evolution: the development of the ability whereby "two individuals perceived and understood a world together, as it were, while not losing their own individual perspectives" (Tomasello, 2020, p. 31). But no matter how well we observe or learn to orient ourselves in the family, and later in larger social contexts, we can never be completely sure of our counterparts: we cannot simply look into each other's heads (and if we could, we would only find biomass there, but no thoughts to read).[17] Therefore, we never know exactly what is going on in the other person's head – every communication could also be intended or understood differently ("He is smiling, but does he really mean it?"). Our inner world is self-contained, thoughts connect to thoughts, but they cannot "penetrate the skullcap", as Peter Fuchs once put it, adding, "You cannot ask someone what he thinks without receiving an answer that is not a thought" (Fuchs, 1993, p. 20). In communication,

---

16 The term "contingency" was originally coined by Talcott Parsons in early systems theory to emphasise that people are inscrutable to one another. It is a difficult and controversial term, and it is used differently in social theory than, for example, in behavioral therapy, where it is understood as the probability that, for example, a reaction or behavior is associated with a reinforcer or another behavior.

17 Whether neurophysiology and -psychology will one day solve the "problem" in their own way is an interesting question. The idea is anything but pleasant – it could destroy the foundations of our existence as social beings.

we can never be sure whether the other person has answered "honestly" (be particularly wary of the phrase "To be honest, ..."). We are ultimately inscrutable to each other – and this is the only reason why we have to learn to trust each other, and why trust always remains a risk.

"Stable order seems, strictly speaking, impossible" (Ortmann, 2003, p. 11); this is true at least for social systems in view of the problem that we are each inscrutable to the other. Humans, as living beings of potentially unlimited complexity, should be very difficult to predict in their actions – and sometimes they are (just visit a kindergarten!). Why, then, does everything in society not just come apart at the seams? Why do we behave in such a coordinated way in many respects? Animals solve problems by instinct and by complex, mostly innate behaviours with which they clarify their relationships with each other, while the "social brain" with which humans are equipped allows much more complex design possibilities (Kriz, 2017b, p. 47 ff.). Here, too, as Kriz emphasises, we have recourse to "organically based categories of meaning". We can access these when it comes to finding our way in different social situations. Consider, for example, "intuitive parenting" (Papoušek & Papoušek, 2002) in which behaviours are applied spontaneously and intuitively as soon as parents are first confronted with their infant[18]. Compared to the animal world, however, social constellations among humans are far more complex and cannot be responded to simply through innate schemas. So how can we explain the fact that we experience billions of frictionless social situations every day across the globe? Children go to school and come back (hopefully) knowing a little more; we go to the bakery and, sure enough, we get bread and not a haircut; we step into big tin boxes and entrust our lives to the pilot – a person we've never met – who usually gets us safely from A to B – all of this usually works. Granted that plenty goes wrong in the world, but probably most processes in social contexts work at least to some extent.

2.2 We are mutually inscrutable

The problem of contingency (i. e. unpredictability/inscrutability) is the starting point of Luhmann's theory: two or more "black boxes" – which are not transparent to each other and which both move in the medium of "sense/mean-

---

18 Even infants rely on *a priori* acquired categories of meaning "which are already laid out in the architecture of the human organism" (Kriz, 2017b, p. 53). Kriz underlines that "a considerable amount of vital meaning predates all conceptuality" (Kriz, 2017b, p. 45). Thus, we are not talking about a purely cognitive theory here!

ing" – start to interact with each other. The ability to create meaning brings new complexity. Whenever we experience, act, or communicate, we engage with *meaning*, not simply with natural processes (Schützeichel, 2004, p. 245) and, thus, uncertainty arises: no one can read the thoughts of another (and if we think a little, we may see this is a good thing!). We know that this is so, and that the other person also knows this: we are doubly inscrutable, hence the term *double contingency* – each is inscrutable to the other.

The continuation of communication is therefore always vulnerable; communication is always unpredictable and inscrutable. Couples can become hopelessly lost in the question: "What are you thinking right now?" because the answer – usually "Um, nothing special!" – never quite satisfies. As "heads are not transparent" (Fuchs, 1993, p. 15), everything could be completely different; we never know exactly how the other person's words or non-verbal communications are *really* meant. Double contingency is, so to speak, the basic problem of social interactions: if we knew exactly what was going on in the other person's head, communication would be unnecessary, and trust and mistrust irrelevant (but how boring our world would be then – and maybe also how dreadful ...).

"Communication is a consequence of the fact that human beings, as biological and psychological entities, cannot coordinate in any other way than by observing each other. The mental system of the one is not transparent to another; thus, they cannot relate to each other directly (even if we sometimes speak of 'exchanging thoughts'). People cannot 'transfer' thoughts among themselves and cannot cognitively shift from consciousness to consciousness. As soon as they mutually observe each other, social processes start, communication [...] begins, which has the basic function of coping with the double contingency of social situations" (Kleve, 2017, p. 355 f.).

While double contingency may give oneself a sense of freedom (we do not have to tell the other person everything, "thoughts are free"), from the perspective of an interaction with another (the other side of the "double contingency coin"), it is experienced as uncertainty ("Does he really mean what he is saying?", "How genuine is her smile?"). As humans, we are continuously concerned with the issue of double contingency in our relationships. Even long-standing intimate relationships are not free of it: we can never be completely sure that our partner will not come home tomorrow and confess that they already have been seeing another person for years, and now want to break up. These things happen; a cherished and assumed expectation of another person is dramatically disappointed. The personal grievances resulting from such kinds of breach of trust are of course often experienced as particularly serious.

2.3 The concept of "expectations"

This example leads us to a concept that corresponds to that of double contingency in systems theory[19] – the notion of *expectation* (e.g. von Ameln, 2004, p. 138 ff.; Luhmann, 1995 p. 267 ff.). To reduce the uncertainty associated with any social situation, people develop ideas that increase the predictability of what they might encounter. They observe each other and draw conclusions about the other's future behaviour; they form *expectational structures* (i.e. expectations that remain stable over time).[20] The accuracy of these expectational structures remains both uncertain and fallible, because, as discussed above, people remain inscrutable to one other. As "talking animals" or "I-sayers", we devise concepts and maps about ourselves and the world that inevitably do not exactly match the real world (Vogd, 2015). Thus, our expectations do not always fit, but to get along with each other, a "consensus fiction" (Hahn, 1983), that is, the idea that we understand each other to some extent, is often enough.

In terms of expectations, we humans 'double' our world, so to speak, and create an image for ourselves of how the world – and thus other people – are or must be, and what we can expect from them: "Expectations [are] condensations of meaning in the form of generalisations" (von Ameln, 2004, p. 139). These expectations create a certain degree of security and enable us to feel at ease in the physical and social world.

We would be completely overwhelmed by the complexity of the world, that is, its impenetrability (=unpredictability), if we did not develop expectations that enable us to orient ourselves. This is a continuous process and runs largely by itself; "Forming expectations is a primitive technique, pure and simple," says Luhmann (1995, p. 268). We only have to imagine coming across a completely unfamiliar group of people. Initially, through our expectations, we "probe" the uncertain terrain. Slowly we become more confident, and the repertoire of behavioral possibilities grows. In the course of "our own history of consciousness," expectations become more and more concise and less arbitrary (Luhmann, 1995, p. 269). However, we can never be completely sure of their accuracy, and disappointment is always possible (and one potential source of conflict).

Expectations can become demands or entitlements at some point; we will address this aspect in more detail later, because this can play a major role in

---

19 Systems theory builds on the concepts of symbolic interactionism here (Mead, 1973, p. 196 ff.).
20 This is true for all meaning-making processes, both psychological and social: "These expectations of expectations form on the one hand the structures of social systems, and on the other hand [...] the structures of mental systems (in the one case this happens in the form of communication, in the other case in the form of consciousness)" (von Ameln, 2004, p. 139).

conflicts. While an initially unmet expectation may be perceived as new information to which we must adjust ("Aha, so that doesn't work here!"), the failure to meet a long-standing expectation, especially if it is now perceived as an entitlement, causes more intense feelings or, as Luhmann observes, "increases the chance and the danger that emotions will form" (Luhmann, 1995, p. 269).[21] The importance of such intense feelings of indignation as a result of unmet demands as a driver for the conflict carousel should not be underestimated.

The word "expectation" might lead us to assume that these processes, while largely unconscious, nevertheless have the potential to be conscious. However, Kriz makes clear once again just how elementary and subconscious the processes concerned can be: developing a viable set of expectations about the order of the world we as living beings find ourselves in is crucial for survival of all creatures, even those that do not have a consciousness in the sense that we do. Thus, "a critical reservation has to be made against the idea [...] that man [...] only defines categorisations through language, culture, rules, etc. There is no doubt that the complexity of the world is considerably reduced by categorisations – but this is also true for the hermit crab or even simpler organisms *before all language*. These seemingly 'distinguish' with their behaviours between day and night, the ebb and flow of tides, or the seasons: in reality, they summarise the immense variety of phenomena in the environment into just such categories" (Kriz, 2017b, p. 70, italics in the original).

2.4 The expectation of expectations

Let us stay with the expectations that are so significant in our social life. It only makes sense to form an expectation if we assume that our counterpart is similar to ourselves. An added element is that the other person also has expectations about us, which we try to anticipate and include in our thinking and our expectations: What might they expect from me? Here we come across an interesting concept, that of the "expectation of expectations", which are "restricted to expectations concerning behavior. No one expects expectations about big ears or noses, the sun or the moon [...] Only the expectation that a person does not show repugnance at the length of someone else's nose can be expected" (Luhmann, 1995, p. 306; see also Mead, 1934/1973). The expectation of expectations, then, is attributed

---

21 Given the role that feelings play in (sociological) systems theory, "danger that emotions will form" is an interesting formulation that points to the fact that the topic of feelings is underrepresented as a blind spot in social systems theory, or rather is considered a disturbing variable (Ciompi, 2004; Raisch, 2022, p. 59f.), more on this in Section 3.1.

to someone who is thought to navigate the same social field of expectations that we ourselves move in. Thus, we have to anticipate the expectations of that other person and assume that they also anticipate that we have expectations of them. "Sociality is [...] not tied to the presence of simple expectations, but to the presence of reciprocal expectations of expectations" (Lindemann, 2006, p. 85).

The whole thing, as already emphasised, should not be understood as if it were about conscious decision-making processes. Sociality starts from the first moment of life: we are born into networks of relationships, in which ideas about what is expected of us are formed even before we are born. We grow up in these networks, develop expectations of our environment, and learn what we can expect from our fellow human beings and what we should expect that will be expected of us. This largely works, as already mentioned, smoothly and silently (although many parents with small children may disagree!) as a kind of leap of faith to make the "fluidity of communication possible" (Luhmann, 1995, p. 307). In other words, we have become accustomed to situations and assume, unthinkingly, what is expected of us.

Especially in everyday public life, expectation structures offer a high degree of regulated stability worldwide: you can assume with a fairly high degree of certainty that, when you sit down in an aeroplane, the pilot will take you safely to your destination; there, you will get into a car labelled "Taxi" with someone you have never met (even if the sign is written in letters you do not understand) and can assume with a high degree of certainty that the driver will behave according to your expectations, just as the taxi driver, in turn, can expect us to behave according to their expectations: our mutual expectations fit. Perhaps this is what makes crime films so appealing: they highlight that social rules, as the "texture of the social" (Ortmann, 2003, p. 12), always include, indeed must include, their own transgression, and in depicting the dangers and consequences of such transgressions, they stabilise both the social rules and the ordering structures of society that the rules uphold: The taxi driver turns out to be a hired mafia criminal who disappoints the passenger's expectation and kidnaps him – and "the gardener is the murderer". It is always exciting when expectations are not fulfilled in a particularly dramatic way – but we may prefer to see these things in a film than experience it in our real life.[22]

Such situations are, however, rare in public life: things usually go smoothly, and if they don't, you just go somewhere else. In closer relationship settings, however, in the family, or at work, where people communicate with each other closely for

---

22 Another story would be a positive disappointment of expectations, which of course also occurs– and then we may prefer to be in the position of the film stars ourselves.

many hours of the day, things are different. The expectation structures between partners, for example, can develop in a tortuous way if both partners deduce from the behaviour of the other that they are not valued, loved or respected.

2.5 A little side view

The processes that are formulated here in the language of the social sciences have their counterparts in other theories. This phenomenon is described in a very similar way from different perspectives. To elaborate on the subtleties of discussions in this broad field is, of course, beyond the scope of this book. I would, however, like to give a short side view of some of the facets of this interesting field. For example, in the psychotherapeutic context, the term "mentalizing" has gained a special meaning, referring to how someone experiences their inner world as distinct from that of other people by empathising with the situation of others (Bateman and Fonagy, 2015). Developmental psychological or neurobiological research similarly assumes the development of a "Theory of Mind": the developing brain may be designed in such a way that, in the course of the person's maturation and history of interactions, it forms assumptions that other people also have their own view of the world, i.e. are capable of adopting perspectives (Tomasello, 2020, p. 124f.). The ability to make cognitive processes themselves the object of observation (to 'think about thinking') is known as metacognition (Förstl, 2012). In this context, I find the evolutionary theory studies of Michael Tomasello, which are closely related to the theory of expectations, particularly impressive. Tomasello, attempted to identify the point at which the development of children diverges from that of monkeys. And the point is quite precisely identifiable, it is *the discovery of the other as a being similar to oneself.* Even monkeys are able to deduce the intentions of another monkey from its line of sight but they remain focused on individual intentionality. The recognition of a *shared intentionality,* on the other hand, is seen very early in humans (Tomasello & Carpenter, 2007). For Tomasello, the greatest evolutionary step made by humans lies in the fact that "[…] individuals are able to create with each other a common agent, a 'we', that makes use of shared intentions, shared knowledge, and shared sociomoral values" (Tomasello, 2020, p. 19). Elsewhere, he describes how this realisation is slowly evolving. Experimental studies show how early the structures of expectation are formed: they examine how the direction of a baby's gaze follows that of an adult, and not only that, but at the same time the baby "comments" on the process through sounds and expressions of emotion. Tomasello illustrates the expectation of expectations beautifully in describing a baby's interaction with an adult: "The baby pays attention not only to the adult's attention to the object, but also to the adult's attention to its own attention in relation to the object and the adult's attention to its attention to the adult's attention with respect to the object, and so on. It is not that the baby explicitly performs this kind of recursive thinking, but it is that the underlying structure of joint attention means that they both know that they are paying attention to the same thing" (Tomasello, 2020, p. 81, translated back from German by the author).

2.6 Relationship disturbances and the metaperspective

The British psychiatrist Ronald Laing addressed the topic of expectations differently by distinguishing between perspective and metaperspective. The second term refers to how one partner assumes that they are seen by the other (which fits well with the topic of "the expectation of expectations"). In an impressive study, he was able to show that the relationships of unhappy couples did not differ from those of happy couples from a concrete perspective (Laing, Philipson & Lee, 1973).

The study design was very unusual for the time: Laing asked each partner to answer from three different perspectives (see Figure 5). The first question referred to the immediate perspective (the first person's view of the second person); the second was aimed at the metaperspective (the first person's belief about the second person's view). The third is a little more difficult to understand, namely, the first person's belief about the second person's view about the first person's view.

The results were interesting and, briefly summarised, looked like this: both happy and unhappy partners answered "yes" to the question of whether they loved the other person. At the next level, however, when asked whether they thought their partner loved them, the groups differed (see Table 1). While the happy ones answered in the affirmative, the unhappy ones expressed doubts. Thus, the difference showed at the level of metaperspective.

Table 1: Result of a study by Laing et al. (1973; own simplified representation).

	"Unhappy" (Clinical Group)	"Happy" (Non-Clinical Group)
"Do you love your partner?"	Yes	Yes
Do you think your partner loves you?"	No	Yes

Figure 5: Metaperspectives (Drawing and copyright: Björn von Schlippe)

Apparently, in social systems where people are unhappy with each other, contingency (inscrutability) is processed in such a way that an individual is not sure whether they can really trust the other person – and so communication patterns of constant testing and confirmation or non-confirmation arise ("If you really loved me, you would have thought to empty the dishwasher!"). Dealing with the expectation of expectations in this way, being constantly on "relationship watch" (Schulz von Thun, 1981) and looking for clues to substantiate one's own distrust probably form perfect building blocks for a "self-organisation of interpersonal unhappiness", illustrated by a statement by Ortman: "People avoid situations in which their standardised expectations may be put to the test. This is a sure way to spurious knowledge – knowledge we think we have because we never test it. Everyone acts compliantly because they mistakenly assume it is expected, and since they [...] never put it to the test, everyone sees their expectations confirmed and mistakes them for knowledge and experience" (Ortmann, 2011, p. 83). A test requires courage, as the result could be rejection by the other person or even confirmation of negative expectations.

In this context, I would like to include a longer quotation from the study by Laing et al. that I think is significant. It depicts the self-organisation of interpersonal unhappiness particularly succinctly and shows that expectation-anticipation (and the anticipation of expectation-anticipation) can cause people to get quite lost, especially in close relationships.

"People are constantly thinking about others and what others think about them and what others think they think about others, and so on. One wonders what is going on in others, one wishes or fears that other people might know what is going on in oneself. For example, a man feels that his wife does not understand him. What can this mean? It could mean that he thinks she doesn't realise that he feels neglected. Or he may think that she doesn't realise that he loves her. He may also think that she thinks he is petty, when all he wants to do is be careful, or that he is cruel when all he wants to do is be firm, or selfish when all he wants to do is not be taken advantage of like a weakling. His wife may believe that he thinks she thinks he is selfish, when all she wants is for him to be a little less reserved. She may think that he thinks that she thinks he is cruel because she feels that he always takes everything she says as an accusation. She may think that he thinks he understands her while she thinks that he has not yet started to see her as a real person, etc. [...]. This kind of spiral develops, for example, whenever two people distrust each other. We do not know how people reach a level of distrust that takes on this formal structure, but we do know that such distrust is common and that it seems at times to be maintained endlessly" (Laing et al., 1973, p. 37 f., in the German version, translated back by the author).

The parallels with the emergence of conflicts are clear here: "Armament spirals between spouses, ethnic groups, nations, companies or departments in organisations take their course and endure because of such punctuations[23] and anticipations" (Ortmann, 2011, p. 33). In a short book that I wrote with Jochen Schweitzer (2019, p. 97 ff.), we show how many systemic interventions relate directly to different levels of expectations and thus provide opportunities for correction or clarification. For example, circular questions, which are common in systemic therapy, ("Why do you think your wife gets angry at you when you don't empty the dishwasher?") explicitly target expectations. Let us say the husband's answer is: "Because she insists on more equality in sharing the housework," then she gets information about what he believes her expec-

---

[23] By punctuation we give structure to the complex flow of communication (Watzlawick, Beavin, and Jackson, 1967). In written language, we do this with punctuation marks, in everyday life by structuring what is said and experienced: "This is the cause of that" (see more in Chapter 6).

tations are. And then when the daughter is asked what she assumes about her mother's expectations and feelings (and her father's assessment of the situation) she might say: "I don't think it's really about the housework, I think she feels left alone, maybe even neglected, and would actually like him to pay more attention to her needs." One can imagine how even just this short interaction could trigger an interesting – and mutually illuminating – exchange about the mutual expectations within the family.

In the systemic method of "sculpting" (Satir, 1988; von Schlippe & Schweitzer, 2015, p. 74 ff.), we navigate the field of expectations by juxtaposing and contrasting different perspectives. Here clients are asked to show their relationship in a "living picture" as if they were a "sculptor". Let us continue thinking about the couple and their daughter Sophie: The husband might be asked to build a sculpture by putting the three bodies together in a way that suits his perspective. Maybe he lets wife and daughter stand close together, and puts himself a bit apart, looking out of the window. How do the "actors" feel: does the picture fit to their feeling? Sophie might respond: "My inner picture is totally different!" and place the parents close to each other. This process and the resulting questions can clarify (to themselves and each other) the different ways in which they see themselves in relation to each other: "Mrs. X, would you have expected your daughter to place you the way that she did? And would you like to show your own picture?"

2.7 Interim summary

The structures of order that underlie our social fabric are a network of complex expectations that help us to navigate the intricate territory of sociality: we behave as we expect to be expected to behave – and that is exactly what we expect from others. Not only that, we sometimes also consciously behave differently from what we think is expected of us (for example, in order to satisfy our need for autonomy) and pay for this with social tension (think, for example, of intra-family conflicts in the context of adolescence).

The overall expectation structures operate not only on the interpersonal level but also on the level of society and culture: the "outer world". Once expectations are regularly met and thus stabilised, they may solidify into demands and entitlements strongly tied to emotions. A failure to meet these demands generates intense feelings, which are conveyed in communication as indignation. Indignation and outrage are the strongest drivers for the carousel of conflicts. This leads us to the next chapter, which will discuss feelings. The experience of the conflict parties and their communications give rise to a reinforcing system of negative reciprocity. Now the negation of the expectations is expected, creating a paradox: If one party behaves in a cooperative and conciliatory manner, thus failing to meet the negative expectation of an expectation, this often is interpreted negatively by the other party. The offer of reconciliation might be perceived as a trick and thus transformed in line with the recipient's negative expectations. This "hostile perception error" is well-known in psychology and we will return to it in Chapter 9.

3 Indignation and outrage: The engine of the carousel

> *"Outrage is the main indicator of social conflicts. Outrage implies the accusation of wrongful action or inaction; the conviction that rightfulness, morality, social rules of common decency, of respect, of justice, or religious rules have been violated, and this by actors, who are seen as responsible for the violation and as not having any convincing reasons to justify their actions [...] The outrage fades when the accused is found to be not responsible for the action, or when convincing justifications are brought to light"* (Montada, 2003, p. 62).

3.1 Feelings in systemic therapy

Systemic therapy focuses primarily on communication and the communication structures within social systems. Feelings were, at least for a time, viewed primarily in terms of their communicative impact. In particular, the so-called Milan School believed that, in therapy, the verb "to be" should be replaced with "to seem" to focus on the various communicative games and their patterns: "Thus, for example, if the father [...] appeared sad in the session, we had to make a real effort not to say that he was sad [...]. Instead, we had to quietly concentrate on observing the effects that such behavior produced in the others" (Selvini Palazzoli, Boscolo, Cecchin, & Prata, 1977, p. 33 f.). The insight of this founding period is certainly that feelings, when expressed verbally or nonverbally, can be seen as communications, and their effects examined accordingly ("What do you think goes on in your daughter's mind when she sees your wife crying?")

Of course, this approach makes some sense: a feeling is always related to a specific context and only comes into play in a social system when it is brought into communication in some way – be it through more or less obvious non-verbal indicators ("What's wrong, you look angry?"), or through explicit statements ("I tell you, I'm just shocked!"). But at that moment, the feeling isn't just a feeling any more. Remember the citation from page 33: "Heads" (and we may add: hearts as well) "are not transparent ... You cannot ask someone what they are thinking without receiving an answer that is not a thought" (Fuchs, 1993, p. 15 and 19). So, we are now dealing not with thoughts and feelings but with *communications* about thoughts and feelings. This is a subtle difference, even though both are, of course, closely connected: "Communicating about emotions is usually accompanied by communicating emotions" (Simon, 2004, p. 120).

The danger of a radical view such as that of Selvini Palazzoli et al. is that it leads one to focus entirely on the consequence of the emotion (Who reacts to the communication in what way?) at the expense of acknowledging the importance of the experience of the feeling itself and the value of encouraging dialogue about it. It may also underestimate the difference between a relaxed discussion about facts and a highly emotionally charged communication, namely that "emotions can provide a different kind of irritation for the social system than logically discursive thoughts or their communication" (Simon, 2004, p. 119). Particularly when we look at the role of indignation or outrage as an affect, an emotion, or a feeling,[24] it is useful to distinguish the experience of outrage from the role that "communicating outrage" plays in escalation. The basic unity of any communication lies in the three-step process, each of which involves a selection (Luhmann, 1995, p. 140 ff.). Selection always implies that something different could have been chosen:

1. Selecting information: from an abundance of inner states, a piece of information to be communicated is selected (it is my anger that I want to communicate, not me feeling neglected, nor bored or sad).
2. Selecting the message[25]: "someone must choose a behavior that expresses this communication. That can occur intentionally or unintentionally" (Luhmann, 1995, p. 140). The information is brought into a form (e.g. I choose just my furrowed brow, and not a thump of the fist on the table; and also not a: "You just can't do that!" – be it said calmly, loudly, or given as a written note).
3. Selecting understanding: "Understanding as the third selection concludes the communicative act" (p. 147): from an abundance of options, a certain interpretation is chosen ("Aha, he's outraged!"; "Oh no, he's putting on a show again!"; "That's typical of him!"), followed by the other person beginning with step one again: one statement connects to the other.

---

24 Affects are physiological reactions that are not reflexively conscious and are more grounded in biology, whereas feelings are linked to the "cultural tool of language" (Kriz, 2017b), so feelings might better be seen as *cultural* phenomena (Stern, 2011, p. 59, citing Damasio).
25 The word "message" is taken from the original translation though it may be argued that "method of transmission" (or even just "transmission") might have been a more appropriate heading for this step.

Thus, a lot of steps are taken (unconsciously) before a felt emotion enters the world of interpersonal communication[26]. Out of a turmoil of emotions we choose one to translate into words or nonverbal signals and the way this is understood then dictates how the discussion continues.

What has been said so far emphasises consciously felt – and perhaps verbally or non-verbally expressed – emotional states. Today we know how much affective exchange also takes place unconsciously, without explicitly going through these loops of information, message, and understanding (Ciompi, 2021, p. 123 ff.). In this context, key findings from this complex field of research should at least be mentioned here:

- Prelinguistic phenomena and those that have no linguistic component, such as the affective attunement between mother and child in the context of baby research (Stern, 2016; 2020);
- The realisation that even infants are able to intuitively grasp the (social) basis of shared intentionality and to move cooperatively within it, which Tomasello sees as the evolutionary advantage of humans over other primates (Tomasello, 2014, 2020; Tomasello & Carpenter, 2007);
- The phenomenon of mirror neurons, discovered towards the end of the last millennium: when a certain intentional movement is observed by a fellow human being, corresponding matching neurons (so-called "mirror neurons") also fire in the brain of the observer (Rizzolatti and Craighero, 2004). This suggests that higher organisms can quickly inform each other about internal states in an intuitive way beyond cognition. Mirror neurons are found in all areas of the brain where experience and behaviour are controlled (Bauer & Marshall, 2009).
- Experienced emotions, cognition and behaviours are stored in memory as integrated feeling, thinking and behaviour programmes ("FTB", in German: FDV, Fühl-, Denk-, Verhaltensprogramme) that guide future behaviour in situations which are experienced as similar or the same (Ciompi, 2004; Ciompi & Tschacher, 2021).

---

26 This led Luhmann to assume that the success of communication is quite unlikely, and that the interesting question for research should be how people nevertheless manage to communicate apparently effectively in so many situations (1995, p. 157). A recent study on the "Extreme illusion of understanding" shows how drastically people underestimate how well they understand and how precisely they are understood (Lau, Geipel, Wu, & Keysar, 2022).

3.2 The little word "should" and the moral demand

Generally speaking – and this is the core message of the first chapters – a conflict can be understood in its broadest sense as the incompatible expectations of two or more parties (Bonacker and Imbusch, 2004, p. 199), which set in motion a spiral of mutual negation. However, something else is needed to understand the acuteness of a conflict, and that is the level of affects and feelings that accompany an unmet expectation – here the factual and relational levels begin to differ (Nagel, 2021, p. 61 ff.). For example, if the couple arguing about a holiday find that they have different expectations ("I want to go to the sea" – "I want to go to the mountains"), a conflict becomes more likely if these expectations are accompanied by a normative demand, whether expressed or unspoken: "But you *should* follow my wishes!" We have already addressed how expectations can turn into demands ("It's my right to ...!"), which are then accompanied by corresponding emotions when they're not fulfilled. Thus, the mutual negation which characterises a conflict is supplied with the emotional energy it needs to intensify. The factual conflict becomes increasingly emotional due to the meaning that is attributed to it, and the judgement and the emotions that are associated with the meaning. "Should" is the key word here – it adds a normative element and a moral demand, because the "expressive order" is experienced as disturbed (Simon, 2012, cites a term by Erving Goffman here on p. 81)[27] and thus also introduces a question of power (who has the right to say "you should!" and make the other concede to their demands?). If this were not so, the negation of the negation on the issue level could quickly be settled: "Okay, then let's see how we solve this, do we want to go to the sea for two weeks first and then go to the mountains?"

However, if the demand is that the second person *should* meet the expectations or standards of the first, the probability of conflict increases. Why *should* they do that? The second person feels that an implicit, normative expectation of dealing with each other has been violated – for example, the one has 'already given so much' while the other person has 'always' tyrannically enforced their own will and 'never' shown consideration – "... and that's enough now!" The topic thus becomes emotionally charged and leads increasingly to this well-known feeling of indignation. This process is accompanied by normative thoughts that increase the outrage: "What a cheek!", "What does she think she is doing? It always has to be her way!", "Does he ever actually show me the slightest bit of consideration?"

---

[27] Expressive order means as much as: people should behave like that! "Due to the behavioral imperative of the expressive order, Goffman argues that the individual 'is expected to go to certain lengths to save the feelings and the face of others present'" (Mote, 2001, p. 225).

The goal of the indignation is clear: the other person is to be persuaded to step down, to make up for the insult inflicted: "Conflicts arise when no agreement can be reached on the valuation of the 'accounts' and everyone tries to 'get their own way'" (Simon, 2012, p. 85). Since both sides generally try to do this in a conflict situation, the symmetric relationship is already predetermined.

3.3 Indignation, outrage and justice

It is worth taking a closer look at the phenomenon of indignation and outrage for it is key to understanding the escalation of conflicts. Indignation is closely connected with attitudes about how another person *should* be, and even more with the dangerous claim that *the world should* be ordered as we expect.[28] This brings us to an essential human motive: justice. When our sense of justice is violated, a particular form of emotion is triggered: the fury "that one feels when one believes that someone (else) is getting something to which he is not entitled. Outrage of this kind is anger about injustice" (Sandel, 2009, p. 14). Everyone knows how inflammatory this outrage is, gradually working itself up into moral sentiment or righteous anger (Kalisch, 2007). Indignant people are convinced that they are completely in the right – one of "the good guys": a conviction that plays a pivotal role in the aggravation of a conflict. At the same time, this emotion is at the centre of an outrage carousel that fuels numerous well-studied psychological mechanisms (Montada, 2003).

Even if most people agree that justice is a noble motive (as politicians never fail to tell us), this moral exaggeration can ultimately have the opposite effect: "Because justice is used in the singular, it seems impossible to the parties involved that there can also be other points of view and that the other side can perhaps also claim justice for its point of view. The rhetoric of justice, however, does not always necessarily contribute to the clarification of the conflict, but often only widens the circle of those affected by the conflict. The strong need for justice [...] does not guarantee peaceful conflict resolution at all; on the contrary, it can intensify and sharpen conflict" (Maes & Schmitt, 2004, p. 192).

The psychology of justice understands justice as an independent motive, a moral imperative (Maes and Schmitt, 2004). Indignation is the response to a violation of this sense of justice. The strength of the indignation indicates

---

28 This does not mean that indignation and the wish that the world should be a better, a more just place than it is at present cannot also be seen very positively (see Chapter 16). I am only trying to point out that indignation and outrage can potentially escalate and thus become dangerous and destructive.

the intensity of the irritation, indeed, presumably an injured sense of justice underlies every conflict, and usually on both sides (Montada, 2000, 2003, 2014; Mikula & Wenzel, 2000). For most people, to live in a world that is just, where everyone gets what is due to them, is a strong need. Even though we humans usually assume that we are rational and objective, in private and when personally affected, "we still believe in the old and deeply internalised story that in the end justice will triumph" (Maes & Schmitt, 2004, p. 188). This "belief in a just world" is, however, a dangerous illusion, indeed a "fundamental delusion" (Lerner, 1980). Justice is an abstraction that can never be fully realised. We can never definitively determine what is objectively just; there are only rules experienced as more or less just or, even better, as "fair" (e. g. "procedural justice", see Bierhoff, 1992). This is because what is fair in each case relates to very different logics and contexts. Thus, two parties can each feel that they have been unjustly treated by the other, become highly indignant about the other and accordingly become involved in fierce conflict, as in the following example (von Schlippe, 2014c; we will relate to this example some more times in the book):

Two brothers, each 50 % joint owners of a family business, were in a severe conflict: both were very angry and felt deeply hurt in their respective sense of justice. One managed the business; the other was a silent partner. They sought support because they had become embroiled in a heated and destructive dispute over the management of the business. One of them, the silent partner, was not satisfied as he wasn't able to determine the direction of the business on an equal footing with his entrepreneurial brother. His demand followed the justice-logic of the family: in their family, particular importance was attached to "absolute equality". The position of the managing brother, on the other hand, was different: "Well, I am the CEO, and I am the one to decide over the company!" His answer was based on the justice-logic of protecting the company's ability to act: the CEO must be able to make decisions on central issues. Neither approach was "wrong" but they were rooted in different and contradictory contexts and logics; both had a justification, but each logic excluded the other's (at least as long as they were not reflected upon).

The need for justice seems to be cross-cultural and universal, especially for those affected by unequal treatment. People all over the world react strongly when they experience injustice. These structures may be already biologically ingrained in us, as suggested by an experiment[29] conducted by the primatologist Frans de Waal (1948–2024) and his collaborator (Brosnan & de Waal, 2003; de Waal, 2017,

---

29 There is an interesting link showing de Waal's experiment: https://www.youtube.com/watch?v=meiU6TxysCg (last accessed 03.05.2023).

p. 284 ff.). Two capuchin monkeys sit side by side in cages; they can see each other. They take it in turns to hand the researcher a small stone from their cage, for which they receive a piece of cucumber as a reward and are happy with it. When the experimenter introduces inequality between the two, however, by rewarding one with a grape, a clearly more popular food, for performing the same task, the other reacts with signs of energetic protest when his expectation of receiving a grape is not met. He throws the piece of cucumber, which he had previously consumed happily, in the researcher's face. Now that he had seen *the other* monkey receive something better, he no longer experienced his own reward as such: "This distinct reaction was certainly the equivalent of what is called 'inequity aversion' in humans [...]. We all know how it feels to get the short straw" (de Waal, 2017, p. 285; see also Brosnan & de Waal, 2003). De Waal concludes that a sense of justice is emotionally determined, "pretty much the opposite of the view [...] that justice was an idea introduced by wise men (founding fathers, revolutionaries, philosophers) after a lifetime of thinking about right, wrong and our place in the universe" (de Waal, 2017, p. 289). We encounter a basic dilemma here: people (and monkeys) react vehemently when they see themselves as being treated unjustly. At the same time, however, *what* is experienced as just or unjust in each case varies greatly from one individual to the next. Indignation thus arises at the interface between affect and emotion, that is, between our *biological* and *cultural* beings: we react violently to injustice, but *what* we individually assess as just or unjust is culturally, and even individually, very different (as we see among siblings).

3.4 Internal account management and justice

It was noted early on in family therapy that family members see their own merits and obligations very differently (Boszormenyi-Nagy & Spark, 1973/1981; Stierlin, 2005). In families, a perception of justice plays a central role. In many cases, members keep a form of "merit accounting" in which each member assesses how they stand in relationship to the most important people around them[30] and, at the same time, closely observes the others to see where they in turn stand in relation to themselves. The resulting "account statements" are unfortunately

---

30 In a very similar way, albeit with a completely different terminology, Lerner (1977) describes how a growing child submits to a "personal contract". In doing so, he or she gives up the needs dictated by the pleasure principle and acquires the claim to be rewarded all the more in the long run. This changes the structure of motives: the child no longer strives to get what he wants, but what he thinks he has deserved. "Observations of injustice and rule-breaking represent threats to the validity of the personal contract" (Maes & Schmitt, 2004, p. 184).

not compared monthly, but they vary accordingly. Of course, everyone tends to emphasise their own contributions. People prefer to tell positive stories about themselves (Bruner, 1997, 1998). And there is another explanation: if we take the well-known difference in the evaluation of the spouses' participation in housework as an example, we can see that it is related to the fact that each was only present during their own activities and was not aware of the time spent by the other: "Oh, you cleaned up the kitchen, how nice!" Interestingly "the perceived fairness of the distribution of housework was more strongly related to partnership satisfaction than the actual division of labour" (Meuwly, Wilhelm, Eicher, & Perrez, 2011, p. 39).

It is therefore always a matter of how a person calculates their own contribution and those of others according to their own logic of justice. It is not uncommon to realise only when the "account statements" are presented how great the differences are. This dilemma becomes particularly clear in the case of inheritance. The "consensus fiction": the idea that others see things roughly the same way as we do (Hahn, 1983), can no longer be maintained at this point. For now, rules *have* to be made, it *has* to be decided who gets the house, who gets the ring, who gets the painting, etc.

Families therefore often find it very difficult to make inheritance arrangements. Unhappy decisions may result in severe family conflict (von Schlippe, 2022a; Wempe, 2022) because family members may refer to very different principles of justice. To illustrate the dilemma a family may face in the case of inheritance, let us take the following fictitious example of an entrepreneurial family (made up of several different families):

"Grandfather William now 82 years old, is considered the real founder. He took over a small company from his father and expanded it considerably over the years, until it had several branches and several hundred employees. The company is in good shape, with no debts. William has always felt fit, but now he is thinking – together with his second wife, Bridget who is a similar age to him, about how he can bequeath the property fairly. It is not simple: he has a total of seven children – two from his first marriage, which lasted only three years, and five from his second and present marriage, which has now lasted 42 years. Most of these children have children of their own and there are already five great-grandchildren between the ages of 2 and 11 (they are listed as '4th generation' so as not to make it too complicated). The ages of the grandchildren range from 40 to 3 years: Anton, the eldest son of Barbara, the daughter from the first marriage, is older than Graham, William's youngest son. Two sons are childless, one of them has an adopted child. Only one of William's seven children (Wolfgang) is active in the company.

Internal account management and justice 53

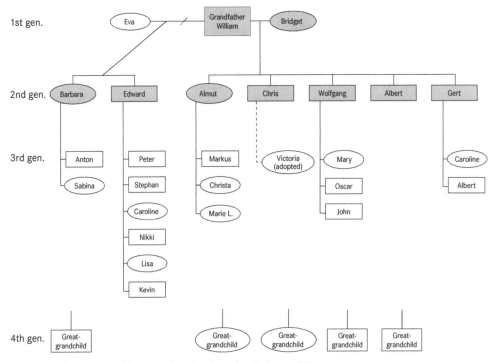

Figure 6: Inheritance problems in a large business family (example)

So far, there have been no inheritance transactions. On the advice of a lawyer, William and his wife Bridget are now considering passing on their shares in the company – but how? Whatever solution is found, someone will feel disadvantaged – and that is something that families usually try to avoid at all costs, but often cannot.

Conceivable variants include the following:
- A 'patriarchal' solution, considered outdated now – fortunately – would allow only the sons to inherit shares. The daughters would be compensated.
- A solution that follows the logic of the company would give Wolfgang, the family member who is active in the company, 100 % of the shares so that he remains capable of acting and pay the others out. In a similar logic (retaining decision-making capacity), 51 % or more of the shares could be given to Wolfgang, and the other half would be distributed among the siblings.
- In line with family logic, all seven children could receive one-seventh each. But Edward, who would have to divide his seventh among his six children, may be unimpressed if the vote of his adopted niece Victoria then carries so much more weight in the next generation than that of each of his children.

- Perhaps it would be fair to give the two children from the first marriage a somewhat smaller share? After all, this marriage only lasted three years, the effective marriage was the second, wasn't it? Perhaps the two children from the first marriage should share one share, the others would then get a whole 1/6 share.
- But no, perhaps it would be better to bequeath the shares directly to the grandchildren (with the side benefit of saving taxes for one generation). Each of the 17 grandchildren then receives an equal share. But those with fewer children will now protest: Albert would go away empty-handed, while Edward's 'tribe' would have more than 1/3 of the shares. Even if William were to distribute his shares equally among all his descendants: children, grandchildren and great-grandchildren, the complaints would not cease" (modified from von Schlippe, 2022a, p. 5 f.).

The example illustrates the number of conceivable logics according to which a "fair distribution" could take place, but none would be fair in every logic. Fischer distinguishes a total of eight different logics of justice in the entertaining thought experiment: "The Goat Case" (C. Fischer, 2019). The story begins like this: "Once upon a time there were three brothers. The oldest, a blacksmith, has 30 goats; the second one, a porter, has 3 goats. The youngest has nothing. His two brothers want to help him and decide that he should become a shepherd. The blacksmith therefore gives him 5 goats, the porter gives him one goat. The blacksmith now owns 25 goats, the porter 2 goats and the youngest 6 goats. After several years, the oldest brother's stock has increased to 50, the middle one's to 10 and the youngest one's to 132. Suddenly, the youngest brother dies. Now the two older ones think about how to divide the 132 goats between them. They cannot come to an agreement. At the suggestion of their aged mother, they turn to the tribal assembly, which considers and discusses various distribution options. Which ones can you think of, that is, according to what criteria could the goats be divided between the brothers? The tribal assembly didn't come to a solution, so the Sultan finally decided to give all sheep to the rich blacksmith as he needed his political support …"

3.5 Are outrage and indignation feelings? About affective-cognitive *"Eigenwelten"*[31]

The response to an injured sense of justice is probably an affective, emotional reaction deeply anchored in us in terms of developmental history. Emotions

---

31 The old German term "Eigenwelten" is difficult to translate. It means that the higher the physical arousal of a person is, the less they relate to the outer world. An inner, very personal world

enable us to orient ourselves quickly and without complicated analyses in complex situations and to be ready for action (Simon, 2004).[32] Their evolutionary sense probably consisted in providing a "response to basic questions of survival" (LeDoux, 1998, p. 135), i.e. to be a powerful motivator for one's actions, especially when fast action was needed: "The path from feeling to action is short, fast, and unreflective. Those who have no time should rely on their feeling; those who have sufficient time can afford careful reflection" (Simon, 2004, p. 133).

What does this mean for outrage and indignation? They are responses to violated values, to perceived injustice, and thus the affective starting point that we have to consider when it comes to conflict. Somewhat more comprehensively, we may say that when elementary expectation structures are violated, an organismic evaluation, that is, an initial affective reaction "on the stage of the body" (Raisch, 2022, p. 24) occurs in the limbic system: "When an emotion grips us, it is because something important, perhaps threatening, is happening, and a large part of the brain's resources is applied to this problem" (LeDoux, 1998, p. 322). Thus, a strong irritation is experienced, as for instance, de Waal's experiment (see the link in Section 3.2) shows: when its expectation of a grape instead of a cucumber is not met, one monkey reacts with such anger and indignation that it even spurns the reward. Viewers who see the short film regularly laugh – a sign that they understand the monkey's emotional state well. Probably everyone is familiar with this strong emotional arousal and has experienced how it has given them the drive to enter an argument: "What a mess! That's it, I'm taking a stand!"

However, if we simply accept our affectively (physiologically) shaped arousal as a *feeling of outrage* and abandon ourselves to it, we have entered a carousel without even reflecting. We overlook an important aspect: affects (the physiological component of emotions) only become nameable feelings through cognitive reflection (Stern, 2011, p. 59 f.), and that means they are closely linked to thinking. It is only through naming that an *affective reaction* becomes a meaningful

---

develops with little or even no connection to the outer reality. A world of its own emerges that tends to stubbornly resist all attempts from outside to change it – the "Eigenwelt".

32 I am aware that I am touching on a large field here which, as briefly outlined in Section 3.1, has been intensively examined in basic theory. In order not to become hopelessly lost in a maze of definitions, I will not further differentiate the subtleties between emotion/affect and feeling, mood or the like here, and will accept a certain lack of precision in thinking about the phenomenon of indignation. To be more specific here would exceed the scope of this book (and my expertise). My main concern is to deconstruct outrage/indignation as a moral instance of justifying one's own behavior in conflict. I refer primarily to Ciompi's logic of affect (1997; 2005, see also Ciompi & Tschacher, 2021) and overview works (for example, Kochinka, 2015; LeDoux, 1998; Rost, 1990).

feeling that can be talked about, processed, understood and through this understanding ultimately, changed (otherwise psychotherapy, for example, would be useless). Emotional and cognitive processes are thus closely interrelated.

This means that what we may think of as an emotion is sometimes rather an intensified affective reaction driven by our thinking. This is exactly the case with outrage or indignation. We all know how closely thoughts and affects are related and the strong emotional charge that thoughts can have. Thus, indignation is not a pure feeling (even if it is experienced as such) but – at least in the human realm – it is closely connected to matching (and indignation-increasing) thought processes (LeDoux, 1998). Luc Ciompi's concept of affect logic – the doctrine of the interaction between feeling and thinking-addresses the close connection between feelings and cognitive processes:

"Emotions are physical-mental reactions of humans to life-important situations that are deeply anchored in our phylogenetic history. They regulate perception and attention as well as memory and thinking. Conscious or unconscious affective moods control the collective thinking in a similar way as the individual one. Their switching and filtering effects lead to the emergence of personality-, group-, and culture-specific affective-cognitive *"Eigenwelten"* [...] that are organised by certain guiding affects and continuously confirm and fortify themselves" (Ciompi & Endert, 2011, p. 13).

There is an intense and circular interplay here: emotions influence thinking and thoughts influence emotions and, importantly, both confirm the other. If we want to understand the dynamics of conflicts, we must be aware of how closely feelings and thoughts interact, influence, and also potentially reinforce each other. Feelings are not always reliable ("Ask your heart yes or no ..."), especially in emotional states resulting from moral evaluation and which are not basal feelings[33] such as fear, hurt, shame or worthlessness are (Raisch, 2022, p. 106 ff.).

Sometimes our feelings also drive us into problematic "dangerous" thoughts (Eidelson & Eidelson, 2003), which in turn aggravate our emotional experience – probably everyone knows what it is like to "talk oneself into rage"; sometimes an observer can have the impression that this even gives a certain pleasure ("And then he still did this and, imagine, soon he will probably also even do that ...!").

"Affect-specific logics" (Ciompi, 2005, p. 75 ff.) lead us into affective-cognitive worlds of our own, which can build up like a whirlwind. Feelings of being affected, the questioning of elementary expectations about how the other *should*

---

[33] Basal feelings (also "basic" or "primary" feelings) are defined as different feelings including fear, anger, sadness, joy/sympathy/love, curiosity/interest and disgust (Ciompi, 2005, p. 79 f.). In the literature, quite a variety of different feelings are listed as being basal feelings (see "Basic needs" in Chapter 8).

be, how the world *should be,* make us susceptible to a "logic of anger" (Ciompi, 2005, pp. 61 f. and 183 ff.) that – similar to a logic of fear, joy or grief:
- acts as a switch and filter on attention, memory and thinking;
- invites simplistic "either/or" distinctions;
- pushes for an immediate, escalating response ("You can't put up with that!"); and
- gives us an unclouded certainty that we are in the right and on the side of the "good guys", so that we can, without hesitation, also act destructively – as "We were forced to do so!", "We had no other choice".

Thus, in outrage, we are dealing with a moral sentiment that is self-perpetuating and self-reinforcing. It "suggests an ad hoc understanding that provides an excuse to put oneself morally above another and to find community within collective anger" (Pörksen, 2019, p. 14). Normative demands increase affective reactions, and the carousel begins to spin. Outrage is closely tied to our notions of – and beliefs about – justice. The world/the other person should be different! Our indignation encourages us to enforce this misbelief at any price.

3.6 A small exercise

This small exercise comes from materials for parental coaching, according to Haim Omer, to help parents manage a high degree of escalation in their family (Omer & von Schlippe, 2023). They are asked to imagine which "buttons" their child would have to "press" (i.e. which actions, which statements) for them to lose their composure immediately. Analogously, in this exercise you can consider for yourself which comments from friends, spouses, children, colleagues or politicians catapult you into feelings of indignation. It is good to take a little time and feel what happens inside when you hear the following sentences:
- "That's not true at all! You lied!"
- "Oh, so typical of you!"
- "Hey, I'm entitled to that, all right?"
- "The well-being of our employees is our top concern!"
- "You're never there when we need you!"
- "You're a fraud!"
- "But what you did there is clearly theft!"
- (Space here left for your own examples)

4 How does communication know where it belongs?

> "When the mosquito heard the lion roar for the first time, she said to the hen, 'He sure has a funny buzz.'
> 'Buzz?!' the hen mused.
> 'What else would it be?' asked the mosquito.
> 'He crows,' replied the hen. 'But you're right, he does it in a funny way.'"
> (Anders, 1988, p. 7)

4.1 The context determines the meaning

In a way it is quite simple: every creature lives in its own 'world'. The schemata according to which they observe the world and the way they communicate within this perceived world are, as in Günther Anders' little fable, basically determined by their species. We may even ask whether their apparent common understanding is an illusion, for the mosquito will presumably think that the hen buzzes very strangely, while the hen might be convinced that the mosquito crows in a rather abnormal way.

Transferring the story to human reality,[34] we can say that the understanding of communication depends on the perceived context in which the communication takes place. The meaning of any communication is determined by this context; by the "field of meaning" in which it moves (Kriz, 2009, p. 622 ff.). It is worth taking a closer look at the concept of *context* if we want to better understand problems of communication – and conflicts are, after all, communication events. Communication is always a joint process of generating *meaning* rather than the simple "transmission" of information, although both parties do not necessarily have to agree on this meaning:

---

34 This interpretation of the fable does not fit exactly, but I liked it as an introduction!

"Communication [...] works with probabilities of possible meanings [...] The receiver receives according to his own processing rules, which the sender can't control!" (Nassehi, 2017, p. 117).[35] These processing rules are co-determined by the logic of the specific context of the situation in which a communication is taking place. A sentence uttered on stage in a theatre – "I hate you, die, you bastard!" – will hardly offend anyone or cause them to call the police, whereas the same sentence spoken in a dark alley by a complete stranger, in the pub by a friend just defeated in chess, or in the marital bed, would open up completely different scenarios. Very different meanings would have been assigned to the sentence depending on the context, as each of these contexts is characterised by a completely different logic. Yet it goes even further, because if we understand contexts only in terms of being "out there somewhere", we overlook the fact that people can also be operating within quite different contexts internally: "You've insulted me!" says one; "I was only joking!" replies the other, indicating that they would like to place their utterance (whatever it was) in a different context. If the other person is already very annoyed, however, they will not accept this and then we will have another – albeit small– ticket for the carousel in our hands.

Communication, as Anders' fable indicates, is not simply a given. It needs to be contextualised in order to be understood. Luhmann once summarised this with reference to internal family communication with the nice question: "How does a communication even know that it belongs in the family and not in the environment?" (Luhmann, 2005, p. 192). Those who would only admit the validity of their own context when it comes to understanding the other person will seldomly succeed in understanding them: communication misfires; goes astray. First of all, we need to recognise that the world looks different from different contexts (i.e. perspectives), and then we need to be willing to place ourselves at least to some extent in the context of the other person. Thus, we can note the following as a conclusion of this section in our conflict notebook: an essential element in the initial clarification phase in the conflict conversation is precisely this question: Is everyone willing to allow the other person to see things from their own point of view and to agree to understand their point of view? It is important to note that understanding the other person's view does

---

35 The German sociologist Armin Nassehi argues impressively against the classical understanding of communication as a process enacted between 'sender' and 'receiver'. It is not about exchanging information, but about complex processes of jointly generating meaning: meaning only emerges when communication is processed, whether the information is correctly understood or misunderstood. Even when misunderstood, a kind of meaning has been created and communication goes on.

not mean having to share it or agree with it – but much will have been gained if they are willing to comprehend the reasoning behind another opinion instead of laughing derisively at such "ridiculous lies" (see also "The art of the unexpected response" in Section 18.1).

4.2 Context markers

So, we see, the meaning of a word, a sentence or a metaphor depends on the context (obvious connections to the method of *reframing* in systemic therapy can be made here, see von Schlippe & Schweitzer, 2015, p. 89 ff.). One of the first people to address the question of how context determines the meaning of communication for the recipient was Gregory Bateson (1972, p. 289 ff.). He saw the context as a "meta-message" by which the "elementary signal" is classified. This sounds more complicated than it is: for example, for the statement, "Hey, bring me a beer!" the context of a pub represents a meta-message that allows the sentence to be understood as an order. At home, the sentence might be understood, depending on the relationship, as an impertinence: "Well, go and get it yourself." The relationship itself is also a kind of meta-message and, if there is any disagreement here, each party will "mark" the context differently with corresponding consequences for the communication – a wife or a husband might react by retorting: "Who do you think I am? I'm not your servant!"; a waiter would rarely answer that way. The word "mark" leads to Bateson's use of the term *"context markers"* (Bateson, 1972, p. 289) to explain that every communication needs additional signals to help the recipient understand where the communication belongs. A uniform increases the likelihood that an order will be obeyed, a smile softens an insult, and a phrase like "The bill, please!" would be met with incomprehension at home because it clearly belongs to the context of a restaurant: "An organism responds to the 'same' stimulus differently in differing contexts, and we must therefore ask about the source of the organism's information ... Certainly in human life and probably in that of many other organisms, there occur signals whose major function is to *classify* context" (Bateson, 1972, p. 289; italics in the original).

4.3 Polycontexturality

Successful communication is thus essentially dependent on orientation to the context in which it belongs. Sentences can have different meanings in different contexts, and there are many different ways to mark contexts, as already mentioned: organisations with their corporate identities marking buildings, uniforms or signs; the atmosphere in a fast-food joint with its neon lights or a candle-lit restaurant, bus stops or railway stations, frowns or smiles etc. Let us go one step further. It is not always clear whether we are situated within only one context at a time – sometimes two or more contexts become muddled. The mathematician Gotthard Günther coined the term "polycontexturality" here to question classical causal notions of a two-value either-or logic (i.e. that something "is" or "is not") (Jansen & Vogd, 2013; Vogd, 2013; Teubner et al., 2011). Every day we deal with complex entanglements of very different contexts and generally have to assume a potential multiple coding of communication. Below, I describe a striking example of polycontextural confusion that I experienced myself a long time ago:

> My Latin teacher was also my chief scoutmaster. As such, we had an informal relationship: as befitted scouts, we called each other by our first names (and used the German familiar form "Du" instead of the more formal "Sie"). At school, in contrast, we addressed each other formally ("Mr B." and "Schlippe"). The one context was clearly marked by boy scout uniforms and tents, the other by regular clothes and the school building. Therefore the two different 'persons'[36] that we were to each other did not get in our way in everyday life: at camp and in scout clothing he was 'Karl-Heinz'; in school, he was Mr B., the teacher. Once, however, I had forgotten my logbook on a trip and needed a signature afterwards – not from the teacher, but from the scout leader! I still remember how difficult it was for me to address him – should I say "Karl-Heinz" (and "Du") or "Mr B." (and "Sie")? It was a laborious scanning of expectations: in the end I went to him after a Latin class and avoided addressing him by name at all by using an awkward passive ("A signature is needed here"). He signed it and helped me out by clearly marking the context: "So, Schlippe, here is your logbook back!" I knew at once as which *person* he saw himself in that context (school context trumps Boy Scout context). I was oriented as to which *person* I had in front of me (example taken from von Schlippe, 2014c, p. 38).

Polycontexturality means "that in a world like ours, no position can be thought of from which everything looks the same" (Nassehi, 2017, p. 19). However, one of the problems in conflicts is that those involved are convinced that only *their* view (i.e. their contextual frame) can be the right one and that whoever denies this must be "stupid, sick or evil" (more on this in Chapter 10). In Nassehi's language, this would be a fatal attempt to counter polycontexturality by "monocontextural forms of description" (Nassehi, 2017, p. 69). In our culture, we move –

---

36 The term 'person' is used in systems theory in a special way, see the following Section 4.4 for an explanation why someone can be two persons within one context.

or more precisely communication moves – in very different system contexts, often simultaneously.

Indeed, this happens every day in many different ways, and we usually navigate these polycontexturalities intuitively and skillfully. Imagine, for example, the communication layers in the complex context of a restaurant visit with your spouse, children, and friends. You speak politely to the waiter: "I would like to have a tea and a water, please" only to address the children almost in the same breath in a completely different tone: "Hey, stop that nonsense over there, and come over here now!" You then adopt a totally different tone again with your spouse: "Can't you keep an eye on the kids? You can see I'm trying to order a drink!" before asking your friends amicably in the next moment: "Where were we? Tell me more about your holidays!" Each of the actors easily recognises which form of communication belongs to which context – tone of voice and body language fit together, and we may expect that, apart from a little annoyance, the Sunday brunch with family and friends will go well.

It becomes more difficult, though, when the contexts are not so easy to reconcile and we are simultaneously exposed to different and sometimes incompatible behavioural expectations – such as the Latin teacher who is also the boy scout leader, but without the context marker of the scout uniform, or a parent who is also managing the family business – how does communication "know" what context is valid when there is a discussion about taking over another company during breakfast? Conflicts are often related to mixed contexts and an imbalance between different roles. We'll look more closely at the problem of polycontexturality, especially in the context of family business where it is often very prominent, in the next section.

4.4 What is a 'system' in social systems theory? An exploration through the lens of family business

Those who are interested in developing a deeper understanding of these processes are invited at this point to take a short trip into the world of family businesses, which will enable us to understand even more clearly what a social system "is" in terms of social systems theory.[37] Business families are, in a sense, masters of polycontexturality. They have to constantly maintain a balance between the communication rules of (at least) three different contexts: family, business and

---

37 If this theoretical insertion seems too complicated, you can skip it without worrying. I would just advise you to at least read the example of the Abel family in this part.

ownership (the so called "three circle model", see Davis, Hampton, & Lansberg, 1997; von Schlippe & Groth, 2023; von Schlippe & Frank, 2013). Each of these contexts creates another social system with different communication logics, so the chance for conflict in these families is quite high (c.f. Kellermanns & Eddleston, 2007; Kidwell, Kellermanns, & Eddleston, 2012; von Schlippe & Rüsen, 2024). What does this mean for understanding social systems?

First, we need to understand that social systems are not composed of people but rather of the type of communication that takes place *between* them (specifically the type of logic that guides the communication). Within each of these systems the people become a different *person*.[38] In this way, a woman can be different *persons* due to different *roles* – founder, mother, boss, partner, manager (and much more) all at once. This can get pretty complicated! Do I address her as my mother or as my boss? In the example of the boy scout and the Latin teacher we clearly saw the problems that the different rules of communication present in different contexts may pose. This is an everyday problem in many family enterprises.

Let's take an example for illustration: a young woman had taken over the family business from her father and had become CEO, while he was still on the advisory board. In a board session, she recounts, her father took out his glasses, saw them being dirty, and handed them over to her saying: "Clean these quickly, will you, please?" Not even the context of a board session could prevent family communication from "breaking into" business communication! In this moment it wasn't simply a problem of roles, the issue was that the father had crossed over into the rules of communication of a different social system that was not appropriate in the current context.

---

[38] Some explanation to the unusual use of some words in systems theory. We need not to go too far into the distinction between *human beings, roles, persons,* and *communication addresses* here. *Roles* are seen as generalised expectations while *person* refers to specified and personally addressed expectations "that can be fulfilled by her and her alone" (Luhmann, 1995, p. 315; 2008). So, the terms *person* and *role* are close to each other, but not identical. A *person* is understood not as a human being but as a construct of communication, as a *communication address*. While a *role* will be addressed mainly in public space (a policeman, a waitress or a barkeeper), in closer contexts it is the *person* who is the address of the communication (you are talking to your one and only mother, not just to a "role"). Luhmann thus makes a clear distinction between *humans* and *persons,* shown in a well-known and provocative quotation: "Persons thus come into being through people's participation in communication. [...] They do not live, they do not think, they are constructions of the communication for purposes of the communication" (Luhmann, 2000, p. 90 f.).

Obviously, something has been going wrong in communication here, hasn't it? Two systems (family and business) were active simultaneously in this case, and in each system, we can find two *persons* depending on the system-logic that rules the communication: in the family system father and daughter usually adhere to family logic, whereas in the business system they interact quite differently as board member and CEO. So, in the example above we are essentially dealing with four *persons*. When one does not pay close attention to which person one is dealing with, i.e. which system-logic is currently "on", communication can quickly get lost. Like in the case of the boy scout and the Latin teacher, it may become unclear which system/which *person* is currently appropriate (a lack of "context markers"), in which case a little "trial and error" may be necessary to come to an agreement. In business families, like in the example, it is a continual challenge to make sure that one is moving within the appropriate system (and the appropriate logic) for the situation (von Schlippe & Rüsen, 2024). From this example we can clearly see "how polycontextural the structure of the modern world is" (Nassehi, 2012, p. 111). Family businesses are a particularly obvious example of the problems of polycontexturality, because of the vast disparity between the type of roles that the members can hold towards each other in this type of context. Let us now continue in understanding what social systems are by taking the example of the following business family:

Let us call them the Abel family: a young man in his mid-20s asks for counselling. Something is wrong in the family: ever since his parents – owners of a small conference hotel – invited him to take over the business, he says, it has been impossible to talk to each other without things getting out of control.

The beginning of the counselling finds a highly stressed family that has been living in a state of escalated conflict for some time. Almost every statement is met with a vehement, highly emotional contradiction. Somehow the communication had become "skewed", but it took some time to understand this. "Skewed communicative connections" are defined as follows: "a communication within the context of 'family' might be understood within the context of 'business' – and if the people involved are not aware of the difference, communicative patterns may arise which can be described as paradoxical or 'skewed'; the expectations from the family and the expectations from the business collide and bring about a certain kind of 'double-bind'" (von Schlippe & Frank, 2017, p. 370). We came to a turning point in this family when we realised that the words "jewel" and "business plan" were continually appearing. They were connected to two situations that helped us to understand the conflict as a problem of polycontexturality. The previous Christmas, the parents had asked the son and his girlfriend to be their successors in running the business. They wanted to hand over their "jewel" – the hotel.

It was an emotional situation, with hugs and tears. When the young couple came back after four weeks and presented their "business plan" to the parents – with suggestions for changing the business and a detailed strategy for the handover – the parents, especially the father, reacted angrily and were deeply hurt. This was not how they had imagined it! The young people, especially the son, felt deeply misunderstood and also offended. Each side attributed negative motives to the other ("What cheek, you want to push us out of the company! You are ungrateful and greedy!" – "Oh, yeah? You didn't mean it at all, you obviously just wanted us as cheap labor, and then maybe after five or six years you would be 'graciously' willing to take us into the company!"). The accusations went as far as insinuations of psychological disturbance ("You're obviously not quite right in the head!").

The dilemma of the family could be better understood by the following exercise, presented here briefly: four chairs were arranged so that one pair faced the other. They symbolised the two logics of the family and the business; thus, the father's chair was put next to the company owner's chair, with the son's chair and the successor's chair opposite.[39] It very quickly became clear that, at Christmas, the two had been sitting in chairs that did not match. There were two men but four *persons* in the room: Abel senior had made his offer quite naturally (to him) from the father's chair (he was the *father person* in that moment), and his communication followed the family logic, so he had addressed the *son person*. But Abel junior had seen himself sitting in the successor's chair (being the *successor person* in that moment) and heard the offer coming from the company owner's chair, made by the *company owner person*. So, to him the "business plan" felt like the right response, whereas his father felt deeply offended by precisely this response because he was "sitting in the other chair" (without, of course, being aware of that fact). The result was that the communication lost its way. The "communicative addresses" didn't match. A communication in the family logic had been answered by one in the business logic, creating "skewed communicative connections". Neither side was aware of this, so they oversimplified the complexity of the events and blamed the situation on the other person: "You are ..." (what you put in the three points afterwards does not really matter!). The result? An escalating conflict.

The previous example perfectly illustrates the greatest challenge that can arise in the context of polycontexturality: communication can get lost when people are not aware which *person* they are addressing and which *person* they are being addressed as in turn. As should have become clear by now, any one *person* can inhabit many

---

[39] I have reconstructed this work in detail with actors that replayed the original conflict in an educational film on conflict in family business (von Schlippe, 2014a) which can be obtained from me (English subtitles).

different social systems, and thus "be" several different *persons* (as communication addresses) simultaneously. In the case above, we see a father and son, but when we focus on the communication taking place between them, we can clearly perceive the presence of two very different systems that are active simultaneously and not separated by contextual markers. Context markers that distinguish when which system is "active" are often less clear in family businesses than in other contexts where work and family are more visibly separated "at the breakfast table company communication will suddenly be activated, or family communication can intercede in the company" (von Schlippe & Frank, 2017, p. 374).

While in this section I have focused almost exclusively on family business to explain what systems are, of course systems and polycontexturality are everywhere, and each of us is likely to have had many experiences of "wearing many hats" – and often all at once. Most of the time, as in the example of the restaurant in the previous section, we handle these processes intuitively well, and there is no problem.

4.5 Conclusion

So, we can now understand clearly that a social system does not "consist" of the people gathered in the room. As a system of meaning it is, rather, characterised by the way in which one communication connects to another in a meaningful way. The respective communications are the elements of social systems. They appear and "once a communication comes into existence it is already gone … Seen like this, a 'system' is a series of communications and the way they connect to each other is always determined by a specific logic" (von Schlippe & Frank, 2017, p. 374). We thus cannot "see" social systems – they are invisible; we can only infer them from the communication, and yet most of us are intuitively capable of understanding the "context markers" of the situation in order to help the communication to not get lost as it navigates between systems and *persons*. It is only when this process becomes skewed that conflict occurs.

Another entry for the conflict notebook: if people do not understand each other, it may be because they are referring to different logics in their way of communicating without being aware of it. The Wittgensteinian suggestion "Look further around you!" (Fischer, 2012, p. 120) may be helpful here.

We may begin by looking at the different contexts in which communication went astray. When we have a hypothesis about this, we can, as in the case study, place the actors on different chairs in order to clarify these differences by artificially creating contextual markers. In this way, we can help the actors not to succumb to the temptation of assigning responsibility or even blame for the misery they all find themselves in by describing the other parties as "stupid, sick or evil".

5 The experienced pressure of causality

> *"Explanatory principles for which simple cause–effect relationships do not apply still represent a significant challenge to 'classical thinking' for many people. By 'classical thinking', I mean that our ideas about how effects can be traced back to certain causes [...] have been developed in our culture within the framework of a scientific programme lasting about 350 years. This programme [...] has permeated our everyday world with its principles. Even when dealing with complicated and complex objects, we can control the world by simple mechanical operations: We can, for example, press the accelerator pedal of a car or [...] operate switches to start washing machines, hobs, lifts or televisions – everywhere we experience this simple connection between cause and effect."* (Kriz, 2017b, p. 124f.)

5.1 Causality – Just a pair of glasses?

The first and perhaps most important aspect when it comes to reflecting on specific mechanisms in order to understand the emergence and intensification of conflicts is the epistemological principle of causality and the inescapable "pressure of experience" that this principle exerts on us (Kriz, 2017b, p. 71). It is second nature to us to try to trace back individual conflict events to "the" cause, where everything started; the original action that caused everything to go wrong! This way of thinking gives us orientation – we know what is to blame, or better still, whose fault it is, and where/who our opponent is: the "tendency to identify a guilty party" is strong (Kriz, 2017b, p. 71). Unfortunately, this simplification usually carries with it the byproduct of increasing social complexity (see also Section 5.2).

If someone is identified as the culprit and the cause of all the misery (and if malicious motives are also attributed to them) and if all this is then communicated ("It's all your fault, because you always .../because you never ..."), this person will usually fight back by refuting the allegations. Furthermore, in the search for a culprit, attention is diverted from the question of possible solutions. It is a dilemma: "Our organs of perception, our language and thus our culture work together here to produce a constellation of expectations according to which there must – quite clearly – always be someone to whom something can be attributed; be it victory, success, defeat or blame. From the perspective of systems theory, however, this form of attribution is something like the essential 'epistemological fall from grace'" (von Schlippe, 2014c, p. 124 ff.).

The question here is: *Where* is causality located? Does it exist "out there" in reality or is it a knowledge tool in our minds that gives us orientation and enables us to act? The answer to this question may be crucial. We are accustomed in our culture, as the above quotation from Kriz makes clear, to thinking of causal connections as objective descriptions of reality (even if they seem absurd from another perspective, such as the growing tendency to believe in conspiracy theories). Of course, the more we take for granted that such descriptions are real and external to ourselves, the more we will believe in them. And such an understanding of causality may often be suitable for the analysis of technical and scientific phenomena – as long as we are not dealing with the uncertainty principle in the context of physics of course (see e.g. Heisenberg, 1955).[40] However, when it comes to conflict situations it could be fatal to assume that only one description can be correct (and when in doubt of course it's always our own one that's the correct one!). It may be quite different if we understand causality as the "scheme of an observer ... There is, in other words, no causality already offered by the world, into which man has only to cunningly insert himself" (Luhmann, 2000, p. 180). Wittgenstein formulates it more starkly: "The belief in the causal nexus is superstition" (Wittgenstein, 1968, p. 63; Tractatus 5.1361).

---

40 We are entering into a scientifically and epistemologically controversial area here. Therefore, I have deliberately confined myself to the question of how causality is understood in interpersonal, conflictual situations; how "certain structures are directly and compellingly experienced in the act of perception" (Kriz, Lück, & Heidbrink, 1987, p. 32) and thus provide us with a self-evident and, in case of conflict, even dangerous certainty. For "in our perception of the world we forget all that we have contributed to this perception" (Varela, 1981, p. 306). Similarly, Wittgenstein notes: "We believe that we are following nature again and again, yet we merely follow the shape through which we look at it" (quoted from Fischer, 2021, p. 19).

5.2 Deeply embedded epistemological patterns

Perhaps, though, the schemata in question here reach even deeper. Perhaps it is not only our culture that encourages us to place causality outside of ourselves. The biologist Rupert Riedl believes that the tendency to break the world down into chains of cause and effect is an innate cognitive schema. For him, there are hereditary ways of looking at things and "innate teachers" that determine the ideas and expectations we have about our world (Riedl, 1981, p. 74). In his view, causality is a structure of cognition bestowed upon us through the course of the development of the human species. Our organs of perception tell us that they can correctly reproduce processes in the external world. However, our innate cognitive structures only provide us with a simplified map, a pair of "glasses" (as Wittgenstein says)[41], which allows us to orient ourselves but nothing more.

Of course, it is possible to find our way in the world with maps that we have acquired over the course of our developmental history, and which help us quite well in simple or moderately complex environments: "Our perceptual and reactional repertoire on the basis of animal brain structures is somewhat local, reduced and 'linear', so more complex systemic connections cannot be 'experienced'. Someone or something is thus perceived as an immediate cause, to which we 'must' respond just as immediately" (Kriz, 2017b, p. 67). This brings us back to the preliminary remark of Chapter 3: The purpose of our epistemological schemata was never to give us a *correct* representation of reality, but "to survive in the struggle for existence and to pass [our] characteristics on to our descendants" (LeDoux, 1998, p. 134). In many ways, the map of causality is very effective. We can represent problems in our imagination, select the tools with which to solve them, and use them effectively (which, by the way, more highly evolved apes are also capable of doing, see Tomasello, 2020, p. 26). However, in highly complex conflictual contexts with multiple influences and circular causalities, using simplified maps and then mistaking them for the landscape itself may lead to disaster (Fischer, 2012; 2021, p. 19 ff.).

This is especially true of mental and social processes, for human behaviour is not determined only by causes but is also influenced by expectations about the future. We do not react directly, causally to an impulse, like a golf ball hit by a club, but first run it through a filter of our past experiences with similar situations. We have expectations about what might happen, we anticipate this and act accordingly – often even with no triggering event behind our actions.

---

41 "The idea sits on our nose like a pair of glasses, and what we look at, we see through them" (cited by Fischer, 2012, p. 149).

In conflict, such causal expectation structures can often be disastrous. Because they are experienced so directly and are not based (only) on thought processes, they expose us to strong experiential pressure and block critical questioning. Our own map is experienced as objective reality, and often defended vigorously against well-meaning voices: "What, you mean that maybe she said that because she feels hurt? You don't know her, she's as cold as ice, she only cares about ..." (Insert appropriate word, be it "power", "money", "keeping the children away from me", "punishing me" etc.).

Over millions of years, epistemological schemata have evolved in us which we rely on especially in situations of uncertainty (the more uncertain and agitated we are, the more easily we fall back on our maps). They always lead us to describe complex factual situations simplistically. When in doubt, the most obvious explanation is that "it" has happened because of the actions of the person directly in front of us. But there are many arguments for understanding causality as a hypothesis, as an innate cognitive scheme according to which we look at the world and which sometimes offers us maps that are too simple for highly complex, interconnected contexts. A softer view of causality may therefore change a conflictual discourse. Instead of insisting on our own explanation, we could take the opportunity to be curious – "Tell me how you think it came to this – and I'll tell you my version!" We can record these thoughts in our conflict notebook as well!

PART TWO:
RIDING THE CAROUSEL – LET'S GO!

As we have explored in the previous chapters, conflicts can be understood as social systems with a certain kind of dynamic. The expectation structures that the participants have developed towards each other have turned negative. The negative disappointment of expectations is now expected. Most of the time both sides experience this disappointment as a strong affront to their sense of justice. On an emotional level this manifests as outrage towards the other party. If these moralistic sentiments find their way into the communication, a conflict system that is increasingly fed by negative expectations and expectations of expectations may emerge. This atmosphere is the fuel and motor of the carousel of outrage. A whole entourage of well-known mechanisms joins the fray. One can see these as "carousel figures", each providing the outrage with more fuel, which in turn fuels the escalation of the conflict. The psychological patterns which dictate the form the escalation takes will be explored in this section.[42] The common denominator of these patterns is that the conflict parties tend to become increasingly absorbed into their own inner worlds;[43] events "outside" serving increasingly merely to fuel internal processes of outrage escalation and its corresponding expression in the "sharpening" of communication.

Of course this all has a lot to do with how we as humans tend to mistake our subjective reality for objective reality, and how conflict warps our perception.

---

42 The individual chapters overlap somewhat. That was unavoidable, however different aspects are emphasized in different chapters.
43 The process, in which parties become submerged in their "Eigenwelten" (see Section 3.5) is sometimes recognisable by the fact that they stop looking at each other, or if they do then only briefly, to take a "snapshot" of the situation in order to subsequently continue to process it internally (more on high-speed communication in Chapter 12).

To deal with conflict in a conscious way means to remain aware of the distorting effects that the long history of humanity and the shorter history of our respective personalities have on our thinking and perception. The question is firstly how we can become conscious of what is happening: to understand what tools of perception we naturally have at our disposal and how these can become distorted in conflict situations. And secondly, the question is how we act within a situation; if we just blindly give in to our patterns or if we are able to remain conscious enough to be aware of the inner world that the conflict is (mis)leading us into. The less we reflect on this process, the more we are subject to the misconception that our personal reality is equivalent to the objective reality.

6 Circularity and punctuation

Figure 7: Punctuation (drawing and copyright: Björn von Schlippe)

6.1 Who started it?

Whether causality "exists" or whether it is a culturally predetermined – or even innate – cognitive scheme (as discussed in Chapter 5) is fortunately only of pragmatic interest at this point. What is clear, however, is that conflict is an area in which the human tendency to search for causal connections is always present. These causal connections may or may not have any relation to reality but will always serve some need: "People constantly interpret reality because these interpretations give them support and structure, reduce complexity and enable follow-up action. In doing so, they tend to reduce complex interconnected relationships to simple, linear-causal chains of effects" (Willemse & von Ameln, 2018, p. 149). This process is known in communication theory as punctuation (Watzlawick, Beavin and Jackson, 1967). That is, people structure events in terms of cause and effect in such a way that each determines a particular point as the beginning of the chain. Each participant structures the communicative process in their own way in order to understand it (Nagel, 2021, p. 57). The stream of words is punctuated: a "punctuation mark" is set both literally and figuratively (Bateson, 1972; Watzlawick et al., 1967; Willemse and von Ameln, 2018) and, just as the positioning of punctuation marks can change the meaning of a sentence, so it can change the perceived meaning of events. As every parent knows, this starts in childhood: "He started it!" – "That's not true, it was her!" (With our own children, incidentally, we as parents liked to interject at this point, "I don't really care who started it. Who will be the first to stop?").

In terms of form, this interaction differs little from the conversation of a couple where one partner punctuates the sequence of events by marking some point in a complex process as the beginning: "It all started when you …" The other usually sees a very different starting point: "Rubbish! I was only reacting to the fact that you …" – "Oh yes, and what happened before that?"

Two parties rarely agree on the cause of the conflict. Conflicts do not arise from nowhere; a situation generally requires a longer chain of interactions and events to reach a point at which it can be called a conflict. In most cases, these chains are so intertwined that it is impossible to clearly identify the starting point because whatever point is set has a history. For example, *he* is naturally unhappy because his wife is angry with him. And, equally naturally, *she* is angry with him because *he* left the flat so untidy again. But *he* only did that because *he* doesn't like *her* bossing him around. And *she* only did that because *she* was annoyed at *him* because it had been so cosy in bed the day before yesterday and then one word from *him* had ruined the whole mood. But that was because ("… as you well know!") *she* had spoiled a beautiful Sunday afternoon before that by making an unkind remark about his mother, but *she* had only made it because *she* was so angry that her mother-in-law had – once again – interfered in how *she* was raising the children, and so on.

We tend to focus on the actions of the person we believe to be at fault, rather than on our own ("When you did/said such and such, I was just totally fed up!"). Especially in conflicts that have already dragged on for some time, communications and actions have a circular relationship: negative expectation structures have become entrenched, there is little movement, and the "punctuation marks" of the story have become rigidly fixed on each side. This was the case, for example, in the relationship between Germany and France before World War II. At that time, the relationship between the two countries was characterised by "inherited enmity", an interesting term indicating that the cause of the conflict had already become obscured (Colin & Demesmay, 2021). The other side is the enemy because they are the enemy; the conflict event is circularly related to itself, punctuated differently from each side. This remains the case today in numerous hotspots of deeply entrenched conflict.

On top of this come assumptions about the true intentions of the opponent – insinuations of motives and projections of what the other may be thinking – which further feed the conflict system (more on this later). The conflict then begins to accelerate, growing apace with the increasing disconnect between reality and imagination/projection on both sides. The best-known and most frequently cited example of punctuation is that offered by Watzlawick et al. (1967) about the man who goes to the pub and his wife who complains (today we might swap the genders). Both attribute their own behaviour to that of the other ("I only ... because you ... "). They punctuate a circular process, each carving their own viewpoint in an ever-deepening groove: the man complains *because she goes to the pub,* she goes to the pub *because he complains,* and so on, ad infinitum. The carousel begins to spin.

The Cuban Missile Crisis of 1962 is a good example of how punctuation can irrevocably determine the understanding of a conflict, and how this may also have dramatic effects.

I remember well the threatening nature of this situation, which I was well aware of even as an eleven-year-old. Since then, in school, in countless conversations, essays and documentaries, the course of events has been presented to me again and again in the same way. For a long time, I assumed that the crisis had been caused, quite clearly, by the behaviour of the Soviet Union. "The Russians" had brought the world to the brink of World War III by attempting to bring nuclear-tipped missiles to Cuba, threatening the United States at close range. Only the decisive intervention of the Americans, especially Kennedy, had saved the world. I only realised much later that this was only one of several possible interpretations and that the punctuation could be placed quite differently. In the summer of 1962, in the middle of the Cold War, the Soviet Union was surrounded by American military bases stretching from Turkey to Japan (Dobbs, 2008, p. 36). Jupiter missiles with a range of over 2000 km were located on the Soviet Union's borders. If we were to take this information as the starting point, we would describe the situation completely differently – with as little or as much claim to validity as the other starting point! Dobbs describes Moscow's attempt to deploy missiles in Cuba not as an attempt to start a war, "but to give the Americans a taste of 'their own medicine'"

(Dobbs, 2008, p. 37). Similarly, by examining the punctuation prevailing in current crises between the East and West, we may come to very different assessments of the situations, as described succinctly, for example, by Krastev and Holmes, (2019, p. 194 ff.). Of course, aggressive behaviour – even if only motivated by self-defence – cannot be justified, especially taking into account Russia's actions nowadays. The example of the Cuban missile crisis shows the enormous power of punctuation: we see how easily one description of a situation can become established as "the truth". Yet in the Western world, too, there is a fine line between objective reporting, one-sided punctuation and an immutable understanding of reality.

One aspect should be emphasised here that is significant both in the example above and to the current global situation. Understanding conflictual processes as circular does not release the actors from taking responsibility for their actions. Any party which behaves destructively within a conflictual vicious circle is responsible for their behaviour and its consequences even if we understand their different point of view. Whoever gives an order to attack or presses the red button bears responsibility for it.

It is the punctuation we add to events that leads us onto the carousel of outrage and indignation, that narrows our view and blinds us to our own part in what is happening. In contrast, we see the other person's part all the more clearly (and perhaps also more mercilessly). Such punctuation is, in a way, a typical "language game" – a concept conceived by Wittgenstein (Das & Neog, 2020), describing an approach, a perspective or a way of looking at things and not to be confused with "reality"! So it is important to become aware of the "conceptual glasses" that we use, as "the categorical imperative of this observation is: look at the whole, look further around you, consider the context ...!" (Fischer, 2012, p. 120).

We continually use mechanisms to reduce world complexity in a way that apparently makes it easier to handle. However, the simplification of a situation we do not fully understand often creates more problems than it solves. Indeed, sometimes simplification increases complexity to ever more threatening levels. We will take a closer look at the topic of simplification at the end of this chapter.

6.2 The paradox of simplification

> *"We are therefore dealing with a paradox: Every simplification increases complexity [...] The simple is not the antithesis of the complex, but a moment of complexity management that contributes to the increase in complexity"* (Baecker, 1999, p. 28).

It is a fairly simple rule of thumb that complexity increases when met with simplification. This rule became known as Ashby's Law of requisite variety. Ashby's thesis is that complexity must be answered with complexity (Ashby, 1991), and only variety can resolve variety (Baecker, 1999, p. 170). The aforementioned argument between the couple about complaining or going to the pub does not become easier to solve through simplistic explanations. On the contrary, it becomes increasingly about who is right in a loop of defence and accusation. The underlying factors – how much time the couple want to spend together, how each can claim space for themselves and how both can shape their relationship in a good way – are sidelined by the attacks. One person is portrayed by the other as stupid or malicious, but naturally sees themselves as blameless. The actors would be surprised by the complexity of the consequences of oversimplification but would probably explain them as being caused by the other person.

At this point, let us remind ourselves that in addressing conflicts it is better to avoid simplistic descriptions of complex relationships as having 'this cause' and 'that effect'. The problem of complexity cannot easily be solved, "but the solutions to complexity can be scrutinized [...] we can ask whether appropriate or oversimplified explanations are used, whether old recipes for success are being held onto for too long, and whether [...] certain causalities are being unjustly ascribed" (Groth, 2017, p. 21).

The question is, rather, of contrasting this with a different kind of complexity, for instance by changing the level of the viewpoints. By inviting the parties to adopt a "reflective position", dialogues about dialogues can be initiated (Drews, Born, & von Schlippe, 2021). As a counsellor, you invite the people concerned "to the balcony" (i.e. to another part of the room) to have a "conversation about the conversation" (see Chapter 20). That is, you take the client to a place from which they can observe themselves from another perspective. This might be achieved, for example, by posing questions such as:
- What kind of conversation are the dialogue partners having right now? Is it mainly 'offence and defence' or do we see other kinds of dialogue here as well (or at least a chance for those kinds of dialogue)?
- Do you feel that the two parties are making progress or is the way they talk just deepening the divide between them?
- If you were an independent consultant to one or the other, what would you recommend that they each do or do not do?

7 Disappointed expectations

Figure 8: Disappointed expectations (drawing and copyright: Björn von Schlippe)

7.1 The power of expectations

The problem of double contingency mentioned in Section 2.1 and 2.2 is basic in systems theory. Because we can't look into each other's head, we have to form mutual expectations about how another person "ticks" in relation to us while they remain inscrutable. In order to orient ourselves and to feel safe with the other person, we observe them in relation to us and form expectations about how they "are".[44] It is, however, in the nature of expectations that they can be disappointed. A disappointment (or disillusionment) is not in itself a bad thing: our expectations (illusions) are corrected and we have a better idea of who or what we are dealing with. Particularly at the beginning of a relationship, we are

---

44 The whole thing happens largely unconsciously and over long periods of time in the context of a relationship of any kind. In addition, these processes are of course quite complex, because they do not refer to one process alone but, rather, to an interconnected web of processes.

quite relaxed when our initial expectations, based on first impressions, prove to be mistaken – someone who appeared so well-groomed (and was even wearing glasses which we took as a sign of intelligence!)[45] turns out to be a little simple-minded. Alternatively, our shock at someone's initial rudeness may dissipate in the course of a longer conversation – "actually, she's quite nice; I didn't think that at first".

Things become more difficult when it comes to expectation structures that have developed over the course of a longer relationship history. As explained before, these involve complex expectations and, more than that, expectations of expectations (what might they expect from me?) and are – whether positive or negative – often well-established. They are no longer questioned; people just live with these consensus fictions, and this can run smoothly for a long time (Hahn, 1983). Only occasionally is a point reached where it becomes clear that the other person may see things, especially the relationship, very differently from us. In the case of a couple, this could be something small like a forgotten wedding anniversary or, more dramatically, a crisis resulting from the discovery that one of the two has secretly been having an affair – the betrayed person is blindsided and had not expected that at all (see the comments in Section 2.2. on double contingency).

In families, disappointed expectations often centre on issues of inheritance (von Schlippe, 2022a; Wempe, 2022). These may be trivial, or less so; approximately one-third of inheritance processes are contentious (Plogstedt, 2008). Those that are serious highlight problematic points in family dynamics: old scores are brought to the table, wounds that were thought long-healed are ripped open, illusions are shattered and old conflicts are reignited. Previously mentioned issues around concepts of justice and morality are brought into sharp focus here.

Expectations are also based on the desire that, if not the world, then at least our immediate vicinity, especially the family (but also the workplace, etc.) *should* be a fair and just place. As described in Chapter 3, disappointed expectations of justice are felt as a strong violation. The theory of social comparison processes (Festinger, 1954) assumes that people compare themselves with their social peers: it is not the abstract amount of an inheritance that is important, but whether one person has received *more* or *less* than another (a sibling, cousin, or friend). This affects an individual's self-esteem and is decisive in whether they perceive a solution to be fair or unfair.

Family members will observe each other and ask how fairly they are treated according to issues such as:

---

45 This tendency to judge a person positively based on them displaying certain traits that we perceive as positive is known in social psychology as the "halo effect".

- Closeness: Who is close to the parents; who feels like the unloved Cinderella or is considered a black sheep or an outcast?
- Settlement of debits and credits: How are one's own services, those provided loyally or those claimed by others, valued? The topic of caring for sick parents in particular highlights rivalry and solidarity between siblings: who has made a special effort for the family or the parents by caring for them? Or has that carer taken advantage to negotiate special conditions for themselves? Perhaps it was all premeditated? (See also Section 3.4).
- The family account: who is seen as less deserving because they caused the parents particular grief, were indifferent to the family, rarely or never came to visit and perhaps even tried to manipulate the parents in their favour? What if he ("Of course, it's him again!") then sits in the front row at the reading of the will and holds out his hand? And who had already received allowances during the parents' lifetime (for example, for building a house, or education) which should "of course" included in the inheritance?
- Disappointed expectations associated with family secrets are particularly difficult to address as they are often intertwined with painful feelings of guilt and shame. "Secrets seem to have an inherent power that is disproportionate to their content" (Imber-Black, 1999, p. 46).[46]

These are examples of how expectations ("What do I expect from the other person?") and expectations of expectations ("How might the other person see me; what do they expect from me?"; for details see Chapter 2) affect relationship systems and also of the conflictual power they release when they are disappointed. The number of families that become estranged (with siblings having no or only highly charged contact) through inheritance conflicts has, to my knowledge, not yet been counted so far but is probably high. In the conflict notebook, it could be noted here that a discussion on different perspectives of justice may have a supportive effect as a "clearing aid" (Stierlin, 2005, p. 89 ff.). "Voice" plays a major role in conflict theory: if each party to the conflict is given the opportunity to present their point of view and be taken seriously, the likelihood of an amicable solution increases (Debra Shapiro & Burris, 2014). So "voice" plays an important role

---

46 As an outsider, it is sometimes impossible to appreciate the intense feelings associated with some family issues. One of the keypersons in Stephen Poljakoff's cinematic masterpiece "Perfect Strangers", Alice, says in this context: "As you know, in all families things happen. From the outside, they may not seem too impossible to solve, not too difficult to fix, but inside the family they have a huge significance."

in reaching "procedural justice" (van der Heyden, Blondel, and Carloc, 2005), of course not only in families.

7.2 Implicit promises: Psychological contracts

Disappointed expectations can be understood through the concept of 'psychological contracts', a term originally coined by Edgar Schein to describe a set of mutual expectations that can arise between an organisation and an individual (Roehling, 1997). However, in my opinion, it can certainly also be applied to conflicts in other contexts (Hülsbeck & von Schlippe, 2018; von Schlippe & Frank, 2017; von Schlippe & Hülsbeck, 2016). For example, take the case of vague promises which at least one person interprets as a reciprocal agreement "given in some form as a promise" (Rousseau, 1995). Often both sides find themselves in this situation unknowingly; in other cases, vague promises are made with manipulative intent (such as a hiring manager saying to the applicant, "I'm

Figure 9: Psychological contracts (drawing and copyright: Björn von Schlippe)

sure we'll come to some satisfactory agreement. Why don't you just start and then we'll take it from there?"). In families, vague comments along the lines of "one day, my dear, you will ..." are commonly made. The problem here is that, for one side at least, this is a binding agreement, taken for granted to the extent that it is never questioned. A rude awakening is thus pre-programmed on at least one side (see Figure 9).

The implicit promises made in the psychological contract lead one of those involved (the one in an inferior position, e.g. the job applicant, child, nephew/niece, grandchild) to take on *obligations* and to link them to corresponding and unspoken *expectations*. They may leave their job or buy a house without clarifying the contractual details. The greatest problem with psychological contracts is that the terms are taken for granted by both sides, each assuming that the other remembers the agreement in the same way as they do. Therefore, it is often never mentioned again, let alone clarified ("Could you please give me that in writing?"). It is then at times of transition (e.g. succession, inheritance, the reading of the will, graduation, marriage) that the psychological contracts are shown to be fragile: "You always said that when I got a business degree, I'd join the company!" – "Well, no, I never said that. I just said that if you studied music, you could forget about succession in the company right away!" Successors in family businesses may thus fall into a "succession trap" having relied on a commitment that proved to be unstable (Kaye, 1996).

From the perspective of expectations and disappointed expectations, these two terms capture what is happening very well: the implicit promise creates an expectation, which is disappointed, perhaps even devalued, when an attempt is made to fulfil it ("How on earth did you get such an idea?"). No wonder that feelings of indignation quickly join our injured sense of justice. Perhaps even stronger than the anger are the feelings of hurt and betrayal.

Interestingly, studies on the significance of psychological contracts in conflicts and their escalation are rare (see Hülsbeck & von Schlippe, 2018). In real-life practice, however, it is clear that their significance is considerable, and since, at least in families and teams, they are rarely used in a targeted and planned manner, a conversation can often help to understand why the other person is so outraged: "Oh, I didn't realise you took it that way!"

In the case of organisations in which psychological contracts are perhaps deliberately used as an instrument of manipulation, it is more important to reflect on the underlying organisational culture, as the damage inflicted by such deception far outweighs the benefits (Robinson & Rousseau, 1994, p. 246). Johannes Siegrist investigated the effects of psychosocial workload, coining the term "occupational gratification crisis" to refer to the feeling that arises when recognition for demonstrated performance is unfairly withheld. Such experiences contribute to a significant reduction in motivation and add to employee sickness, absenteeism from work and early retirement due to sickness (Elovainio, Kivimäki, & Vahtera, 2002; Siegrist, 2000). The issue should not be taken lightly: Siegrist cites a representative sample of employees in Germany of which 37 % feel their pay is unfair and not commensurate with services rendered; similar figures are reported by Zhao, Wayne, Glibkowski, & Bravo (2007) in other contexts.

7.3 Disappointed expectations and the "deep story"

So far, the concept of expectation has been considered predominantly on an immediate and interpersonal level: what do people expect from each other? We will now briefly consider how we might imagine expectation structures on a different level and how these levels can then also become significant on a small scale in people's everyday lives using the example of a study by the American sociologist Arlie Hochschild (Hochschild, 2018). Hochschild, professor emerita of sociology at Berkeley, had the ambition to overcome the "empathy wall" that separated her – a democratically-minded and enlightened US citizen – from Tea Party voters, especially in the southern states. She sees this division as the cause of increasing hostility in the US (the study was conducted during the tenure of President Obama; today the situation has only intensified).

Hochschild always gives her full personal commitment to her studies, as also in this case. After a friend of her mother put her in contact with people close to the Tea Party, she spent a total of five years in Louisiana, one of the poorest states in the US despite its great oil wealth. She describes her experiences in the first part of the study, reporting moving encounters with often deeply religious people who had worked hard all their lives in small businesses or as self-employed workers, but who today can only make ends meet with second or even third jobs. They become sad when telling of their nature-loving childhoods, of catching crayfish with their fathers in the river, in areas that are now ecologically dead as a result of oil production and pollution. Hochschild faces this paradox: these people oppose regulations on labour, oppose stricter environmental laws and think talk of climate change is nonsense. How can it be explained that residents of a county "with higher pollution levels [are] more likely to think Americans 'worry too much' about the environment and that the United States does 'more than enough' for them" (Hochschild, 2018; all citations translated back from German by the author)? At the same time, these same people vote for a party that stands for policies that make the foundations of their lives increasingly precarious. To unravel this contradiction, Hochschild argues, we need to understand the whole story – and this brings us back to the issue of expectations and disappointed expectations. The whole story, according to her study, is a "felt view of things [...] It hides judgment and facts and tells how things feel [...] we all have a deep story" (Hochschild, 2018). She refers here to the underlying narrative that governs our lives and that we must recognise if we are to understand. Her study attempts to reconstruct the underlying narrative of this population; in each case, her reflections were presented to and confirmed by those affected. To illustrate her point, she chooses the metaphor of a drama in several acts. The first act is called "Queuing": "You wait patiently in a long line that [...] leads up a mountain. You stand in the middle of this line along with others who are also white older Christians and a majority of them men [...] Just beyond the top of the mountain is the American Dream, the goal of all those waiting in line. In the back [...] are many people of color – poor, young, and old" (Hochschild, 2018).

What is the goal at stake? The promise of the American Dream has created an expectation – "Anyone – including me – can make it if they just play by the rules!" For a long time, people have trusted this promise, but now the second act, "The Queue Jumpers", has begun. Suddenly, people are jumping to the front of the queue – people of colour, for example, who are taking advantage of government-imposed anti-discrimination measures to obtain preferential treatment, women, refugees, immigrants – all these are given opportunities denied to the original group and use them to push their way in front. Even a brown pelican with oil-stained wings pushes its way to the front of the line – it's just not right!

Frustration grows; people become suspicious. So, the next act is entitled "Betrayal". Who is helping these pushers? They obviously have powerful friends that you do not have yourself – a president like Obama is clearly on the side of the pushers or, at least, he is certainly not on the side of "decent Americans"! Slowly, people become convinced of betrayal and webs of lies everywhere; the more they feel socially sidelined, the greater the feeling of being "strangers in their own country" (the title of the book).

This felt story of betrayal and the favouring of others by impenetrable political structures offer, for Hochschild, an explanation of contemporary phenomena that are so difficult to comprehend. This underlying emotional story with its sense of betrayal is exploited and instrumentalised by certain political forces and was, in Hochschild's view, the optimal prerequisite for the election of Donald Trump (Hochschild, 2016), who skilfully posed as a spokesman for the ordinary person, "I am your voice!" It is not difficult either to relate the idea of an "underlying history of expectations" to the tense relationship between East and West

Germany against the failure to live up to expectations associated with the image of "blooming landscapes", a phrase coined by chancellor Helmut Kohl in 1990 as a metaphor for his hopes for the future of a united Germany after the fall of the Iron Curtain. Even if no solution to complex problems can be presented at this point, an understanding of the underlying story can help to clarify the seemingly paradoxical behaviour of people in conflict situations, not only in the relatively manageable interpersonal sphere, where they become recognisable as psychological contracts, but also in conflicts between population groups. This feeling of betrayal at the level of the whole story, where many basic expectations are found, is likely to explain destructive behaviour in small and large conflict situations.

7.4 The implicit relationship contract in couples

In conflict work with couples, the question of psychological contracts and the "deep story" of the partners' (disappointed) expectations of each other can be helpful in understanding current conflict. This is about the implicit relationship contract, which is usually made unconsciously as the couple formed. The dynamics of such a "contract" can determine the course of the relationship in a similar way to those of a psychological contract; in particular, the partners' disappointments about each other can often be related to it.

One way to approach this relationship contract and understand the underlying story that influences the couple's dynamics is to ask about the "opening gambit".[47] In chess, the term is used to describe the opening move, which usually has a strong influence on the course of the game. In the early phase of a relationship, the rules for future cooperation are negotiated unconsciously. Even the opening move may symbolise the ups and downs of the later relationship, forming the implicit relationship contract that often leads a couple to counselling much later. For example:

Three days after getting to know each other, a couple sit under a tree in the sun. Playfully, he turns his partner's ring around so that it looks like a wedding band. She then asks, "May I now consider myself engaged?" Afraid to say that it is too early for him to answer this question, his half-hearted yes lays the groundwork for a long-standing feeling of being "trapped"; for her, it goes hand in hand with the long-standing feeling of having to hold him close and never being quite sure of him.

---

47 I owe these considerations in large part to my esteemed Heidelberg colleague Barbara Brink, who sadly passed away at an early age.

Asking about a significant key scene in the early days of the relationship can be revealing. This might be:
- the first meeting
- the first time one gave the other the key to their apartment
- the first sexual encounter and the reactions to it
- the first time that money issues arose (who pays at a restaurant?).

At these moments, especially if they are remembered as significant (sometimes only by one party), the expectations one person has of the other are condensed in the implicit relationship contract, and perhaps also the first disappointments (for example, after the first night spent together when one person says to the other, "But that doesn't mean much to both of us, does it?"). Both can be asked about the ideas, hopes and desires they took into the relationship (usually without ever explicitly addressing this). It can be helpful to consider these questions separately, for example, as part of a homework assignment, and to discuss them in the next session.

These scenes can thus be used as a key to understanding the underlying story, the "deep story", of the couple and may initially help both parties to better understand the other's reactions. In a further step, the couple can then be asked how meaningful their implicit contract is for their relationship today and whether it should be renegotiated.

8 Hit where it hurts: Experience and self-esteem

Figure 10: Self-esteem in need (drawing and copyright: Björn von Schlippe)

> *"Recurring conflicts almost always have to do with appreciation. This is not to say that the issues being argued about are not important. In fact, they are often very important. But when partners do not have to worry about their self-esteem, they can usually talk reasonably about their disagreements"* (Catherall, 2022, p. 39).

The phenomena described so far become significant on the level of the social system, that is, in communication. Communication is in turn, however, also an important factor in the individual's "inner experience". Everything that is communicated verbally and non-verbally has an effect (a "resonance") on the inner emotional experience of those involved and this resonance, in turn, pervades each resulting external communication and affects the self-esteem of the recipient (Satir, 1988). The "internal" and "external" are connected but not causally. Communication is not directly transmitted into the receiver's mind; thoughts can only be transmitted in a modified form through verbal and non-verbal processes at which point they are no longer thoughts (see Chapter 1) in which the listener assigns meaning to what has been said. The concept of resonance perhaps fits best here; internal and external (communicative) processes are closely interconnected: "Meaning can be understood only in context, and context is, initially, supplied by one's own perceptual field and memory" (Luhmann, 1995, p. 158; see also 4.2, especially the quotation from Bateson at the end of 4.2).

What is expressed here in a somewhat complicated way is familiar to us all: "How can you say something like that?" (the question is framed negatively by the dialogue partner; indignation rises). "Come on, I was just kidding. Sorry, I didn't mean to offend you!" (the speaker frames their statement differently: as a joke, soothing the indignation). "All right, but next time be careful what you say." The problem is resolved because the listener realises that the first person did not mean the statement in the way that they had interpreted it. Unfortunately, it is not always so easy to resolve such issues.

One particular area in which self-esteem is often strongly affected is within closed (incongruent) communication: the internal (how we feel) and the external (what we say or do) often do not match (creating incongruence). The listener feels threatened and their self-worth devalued, but instead of expressing these feelings, they react in such a way that the speaker feels threatened in turn. This can lead to a "malignant clinch" in conflict: Both interpret the behaviour of the other as a threat and take this as a reason to defend themselves, whereby the expectations with which each of the parties involved enter into the conflict tend to confirm themselves.

Thus, the many ambivalences, attacks, devaluations and ambiguities with which the actors are confronted in a conflict increase the likelihood that they will feel insecure, misunderstood and, above all, hit in their self-esteem. As a result, communication becomes increasingly incongruent because, in conflict, the actors engage more in saving face than in arguing the matter at hand. The American family therapist Virginia Satir saw an attempt to defend oneself and hide low self-esteem behind many dysfunctional forms of communication. She distinguished between the accusatory, the soothing, the rationalising and the distracting forms. In each form, communication becomes incongruent because the parties are more concerned with defending themselves than with talking openly (congruently) about what they are feeling (Satir, 1988).

Sometimes, when a person feels attacked and devalued, "auxiliary engines" from their personal history start to kick in (Schulz von Thun, 1981; see Figure 11), which do their part to make them feel even worse: "I have never ..."; "I am completely useless ..."; "She has always ..."; "You are just like (insert name)".

If we take a closer look at the vicious circle, we can distinguish the various driving forces that are exacerbated by the carousel of outrage:

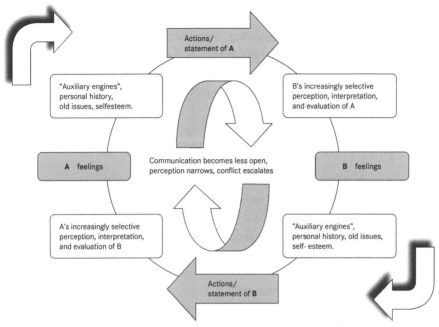

Figure 11: Self-esteem, communication and escalation (own presentation from von Schlippe, 2014c, p. 133, based on Schulz von Thun)[48]

- narrowed perception, e.g. "I don't remember what he said, but I remember *the way he looked*: I knew exactly what he was up to!" (See also Chapters 9 and 12);
- interpretation made in the context of fixed expectations, which suggest simple causal relationships or fantasies about the motives of the other person, e.g. "Now she wants to finish me off again – but I'm not going to let her get away with it!";
- individual, personal "auxiliary engines" that stabilise the sense of self-worth. These may be a personal story, for example, resolutions such as "Never again will I let anyone …" or specific words that trigger old and familiar negative emotions, which may then turn into violent feelings that are disproportionate to the situation (vicious circles can be observed particularly well here) and
- an accelerated dynamic of fast turn-taking in communication, which can be so sudden that neither partner can leave the conflict, even with the best of intentions. An observer may feel like a referee in a tennis match, switching back and forth between the parties involved as the exchange escalates.

---

48 Similarly, see also Ballreich and Glasl (2011, p. 270 f).

Example:
A married couple comes for counselling. Both complain that trivial disagreements become heated arguments in no time at all, which they both find destructive. In a recent example, they describe how the wife (A) had asked her husband (B) to fetch the mineral water from the cellar. A reconstruction of this typical situation shows the vicious circle as follows:

A'S STATEMENT (WOMAN): "Get some water from the cellar, please!"

B'S PERCEPTION (MAN): That sharpness in her voice!
B'S INTERPRETATION: She talks to me so harshly. She wants to bully me again!
B'S FEELINGS: anger, annoyance
B'S AUXILIARY ENGINES (elaborated in counselling later): an old feeling of "I'm always being bulldozed, and I'm sick and tired of it!"

B'S STATEMENT: "Go and get it yourself!"

A'S PERCEPTION: The way he looks at me when he says that!
A'S INTERPRETATION: He rejects me, leaves me hanging again, doesn't see how tired I am, doesn't love me!
A'S FEELINGS: abandoned, used.
A'S AUXILIARY ENGINES: the old feeling of "I never get what I need! In the end, I'm always on my own."

A'S STATEMENT: "That's the last straw! If this carries on, I'd be better off alone!"

We can imagine what happens next. Both partners react with strong feelings that fuel the dynamics. These feelings are fed by old individual auxiliary engines which, together with the universal statements "always" and "never", ensure that the situation escalates quickly and far out of proportion to the apparent occasion (see Chapters 9-12).

In an atmosphere of tension and irritation, the likelihood of misunderstandings increases, and these affect perceptions in the way described. Escalating vicious circles take on a life of their own; the conflict becomes increasingly distanced from the issue at hand and turns from "tasks" and "processes" into "relationship conflict" (see Chapter 1). The decisive point at which a conflict about facts turns into one about the relationship is the moment when, for the first time, factual arguments are replaced by an attack on the "face" of the other, on their self-esteem: "Are you so stupid that you don't get it?" On Glasl's (2014b) nine-level scale of conflict escalation (discussed in detail in Chapter 15),[49] this occurs at Levels 4–5. The fifth level is entitled "loss of face". Glasl writes, "In hostile confrontations, targeted public defamatory attacks occur in which the trustworthiness of the opponent is denied" (Glasl, 2014b, p. 191). It is precisely at this point that the conflict becomes more acute; it is now less about the matter at hand and more about fending off an attack on one's self-esteem.

For every human being, emotional security is a prerequisite for optimal functioning and well-being. Communication and affective mood resonate positively with each other. Catherall (2022, p. 98 ff.) also speaks of the "power of affective resonance" (with reference to couples). In this context, he quotes Susan Johnson as saying, "The affective mood is more important than the content of the dialogue" (p. 101). To some degree, this may also apply to families, groups or larger collectives. The preservation of self-esteem is considered a basic psychological need and conflict comes close to violating this basic need. Various approaches are used to define basic needs, with some key differences, but in practice, the question of which needs and emotions are seen as "basic" is a very personal one. For John Burton, who was mainly concerned with large-scale international conflict, basic needs include security, distinctive identity, the social recognition of identity and effective participation in determining development requirements (Fisher, 1990, p. 147, see also Burton, 1993). The German researcher Klaus Grawe, in contrast, described self-esteem, attachment, orientation, control and pleasure (and the avoidance of unpleasant experiences) as basic needs (Fries and Grawe, 2006). The need for attachment fits well with the "need to belong" that Baumeister and Leary (1995) see as central. The Harvard model of conflict management (see Chapter 19) cites the following basic needs:
- *Autonomy:* the need to make one's own decisions and be in control of one's own destiny,
- *Recognition:* the need to be recognised and appreciated by others,
- *Connectedness:* the need to be recognised as a member of a group,
- *Role:* the need to perform a meaningful task, and
- *Status:* the need to be fairly valued and recognised (Fisher, Ury, & Patton, 2019, p. 62, translated back from the German version by the author).

It is easy to understand that in escalated conflicts basic needs other than self-esteem are also questioned to a greater or lesser extent, so that the person affected enters a state of alarm that affects thinking, perception and memory. While an

---

49 Since the last escalation stage of the stage model is titled "Together into the abyss", I have placed the model at the end of the carousel in Section 15.1.

individual moves in an "everyday logic" when coping with everyday tasks, they enter into an "anger logic", a "fear logic", a "grief logic" (Ciompi, 1997; Ciompi & Endert, 2011) or even a "self-esteem defence logic" with increasing arousal.

Perhaps it would be more appropriate to speak of "shame logic" when it comes to attacks on "face", for this feeling should not be underestimated in this context.[50] Shame is caused when a core boundary is violated, as is regularly the case in escalating conflicts. Derisive remarks, humiliating gestures and devaluation are conflict strategies in highly escalated conflicts. Shame is a particularly harmful feeling because it is experienced as a profound questioning of one's core sense of self.

Shame is a sign of dysfunction in one's relationship with another person or people and a very powerful "motivator" (Catherall, 2022, p. 113). At the same time, it is a very intimate feeling because it has to do with the relationship a person has with themselves: if they are ashamed, they can no longer see themselves as valuable. Thus, shame makes it difficult for the shamed person to approach the other person again (Weinblatt, 2013, 2016; 2018).

When shame is involved, therefore, defence becomes strong. These defensive reactions are sometimes difficult to connect to shame as they are part of a strategy to hide feelings of shame (especially in an environment of conflict and struggle). The masking of shame can, for example, take the form of turning it into the opposite – hiding behind impudence (as experienced more often among adolescents), aggression and attacks on the self-worth of the other person, but also in withdrawal, coldness and silence.

A person who does not feel recognised and appreciated will of course also deny the other party this recognition. The devalued person defends himself against feelings of shame by devaluing the other. Ciompi speaks of the "shame-rage spiral": If suppression does not succeed and the emotional tension continues to rise, initial feelings of shame and depression may frequently turn into anger or envy and an aggressive desire for revenge [...], which in an effort to restore the damaged self-esteem are eventually released as open aggression and violent actions [...]. Feelings of triumph and superiority arising from this basis can grow to become arrogance, accompanied by delusions of grandeur [...], which in turn lead to the humiliation of the defeated enemy and thereby set new shame-rage spirals in motion" (Ciompi, unpublished remark).

---

50 It is undisputed that shame also has a positive function in making us aware of when we transgress elementary familial, partnership, or societal rules (Catherall, 2022; Marks, 2013; Weinblatt, 2018). Here, we will focus exclusively on the "unhealthy shame" that results from boundary transgressions.

Thus, "shame often hides behind anger" (Weinblatt, 2016, p. 18) and sometimes a leap is made from shame to violence, whether psychological or physical (Marks, 2013).

At this point, if not before, the dynamics of the conflict take on a special quality: the struggle is no longer about winning (although that usually remains a part of it) but is now above all about *not* losing, *not* being ashamed and *not* being the fool. The close link between the conflict, our vital self-esteem and the existential need to protect ourselves from embarrassment can lead to a particular intensity in the conflict. When a conflict grows to this level, it often creates a feeling that our entire existence is at stake.[51]

This feeling creates a particular challenge in conflict moderation. The key is to speak in such a way that the self-esteem of all participants remains intact. The above-mentioned family therapist Virginia Satir specifically emphasised this topic in her work (Satir, 1988), as illustrated in the following short example. In conversation with a family, Satir began by asking everyone their name and writing it on a chart. She then asked if they were willing to give their age and wrote that next to their name. She then wrote her own name and age underneath. To the amazement of the family, she added up all the ages: "186 years of life experience are gathered here in this room so it would be pretty silly if we could not manage to discuss all the worries that brought you here in a productive and friendly manner!" (quoted from memory) – a brilliant way of defining the therapeutic system, in which she included herself, in an anxiety-free cooperative setting.

It is a simple but impactful exercise. In conflictual systems we often see a "seesaw of self-esteem", a kind of "zero-sum game": one person's self-esteem is increased by depreciating that of the other. These "games" are designed such that one person's gain inevitably means the other's loss, as in chess but also war. The art of moderation is to transform the seesaw game of self-esteem into one in which both sides can benefit from cooperation.

A small entry for the conflict notebook: The friendly recognition of every individual and a comprehensive look at the resources that might be found in the conflict system are, beyond all methodologies, the best foundations if you want to help the carousel to slow down.

---

51 At the extreme, this is likely the point at which one is ready to take the other party to go down "into the abyss together" – the last stage of Glasl's escalation ladder discussed in Section 15.1.

9 The one-sided view: Perception in conflict

Figure 12: The one-sided view (drawing and copyright: Björn von Schlippe)

We constantly try to explain the actions of our fellow humans: we want to understand our social environment and find it predictable so that we feel safe(er) (see Chapter 2). The more complex our environment and the more we feel under stress, the more we want the world to be "in order" and to feel that we are in control. To understand what is happening around us, we unconsciously apply search strategies, so-called "heuristics", because no one has all the information they need about a given situation. We cannot help but be selective, to make decisions and evaluate facts on an incomplete basis. We do this automatically, barely thinking about it – and in many everyday situations, it works well. However, if our heuristics send us in the wrong direction, especially in the case of conflict, it requires energy and motivation on our part to switch to conscious thinking.

The urge to feel safe in the knowledge that our map is correct is sometimes so important to us that we no longer even ask to what extent it matches the landscape it is supposed to represent. Yet some of the pathways drawn on these maps may lead directly to an intensification of the conflict. For example, they may be based on broad assumptions about social reality, often completely misrepresenting the position of others while making us blind to our own part in the conflict. The following section describes certain mechanisms which have been frequently studied within the field of psychology but which are not more widely known. It may be helpful to be aware of their effects in conflict situations.

9.1 The one-sided view (Part 1): Person-related attribution and motive attribution

Let us start with two popular heuristics often used to try to grasp the complexity of social processes: *"person-related attribution"* – i.e. attributing the causes of a conflict to a person (or group) and the associated tendency to make assumptions about the motives behind that person's actions in order to interpret their behaviour (*"motive attribution"*) – "He does that because ...". Both ways to build a map of the situation can, from a systemic point of view, be called "a first fall from grace" (von Schlippe, 2014c, p. 126), because they lead straight to escalation.

Attributing the cause of the conflict to the other party may seem inevitable since it is usually the other person's behaviour that has caused us to become angry, upset or indignant. However, asking questions such as the following would perhaps do more justice to the complexity of conflict situations:
- What other contextual factors may need to be considered (keyword "polycontexturality" from Section 4.3)?
- What might our own possible contribution look like?
- How might possible "conciliatory inner voices" (our own or the opponent's) be found?
- What interests might be found behind the strong positions that our opponents are adopting (see Chapter 19)?

Asking questions like these would perhaps give us a better chance of understanding the complexity of conflict situations. Since they are more difficult to answer, however, they tend to remain unasked and unanswered. We believe it is the other party's fault and that is the end of the matter. The causal relationship seems obvious to us: if only *they* would behave differently, everything would be simple, but because *they* did/said/made [insert any grievance], we are in this situation! The explanation is simple, but at the same time it is an important stage on the carousel, especially when combined with the second pattern – "motive attribution". Here, one thing is clear: the other party is to blame. The explanations chosen in each case are often full of lay psychology ("simple motive attributions"): "He wants to undermine my authority because he's scared of me ..."; "I bet she's going to try to stop me from getting a promotion because she's just jealous/envious/greedy/spiteful, etc."). Sometimes, among those with some rudimentary knowledge of psychology, motives attributed may take on a more "advanced" form of "pop psychology" (see Figure 11): "I know that he suffered from ... in childhood, and therefore he ..."; "Basically he never got over the fact that his mother left him ... and that's why," until finally, as the conflict escalates and the thinking simplifies accordingly (see Chapter 10), "She's just plain crazy – she really should see a psychiatrist!"

An unintended side effect of attributing motives is that they invite negative reciprocity. For rarely does one put up with the other person "trying to get into one's head or even one's soul" thinking that they "know" what's really going on in there. Thus, motive attribution is often countered with an equivalent but opposite attribution ("You're only saying that because you want to distract from the fact that, in reality, it's you who has the unresolved problems!"). Thus, the attempt to reduce complexity (we've identified the culprit) results in increased complexity; the effects grow and, fighting to save face (see Chapters 8 and 15), the parties become sucked into vicious circles of accusations and counter-accusations. While it is "anything but easy to switch from this type of person-related attribution to thinking in terms of expectation structures and communicative patterns, especially if one is part of this pattern oneself" (von Schlippe, 2014c, p. 127), it is probably necessary to do so if we seriously want to work on conflict resolution. However, should this not be the case, you are welcome to make use of the construction kit shown below to add fuel to the fire! (see Figure 13).

The observation: an unwanted behaviour	The person-related attribution	The simple motive attribution	The advanced motive attribution, backed up by pop psychology
The key is not where it should be ...	... of course, I bet it's you who forgot it again, typical ...	... you do that again and again on purpose, to get one over on me ...	... and that shows you still haven't resolved your issue with your mother!

Figure 13: Attribution toolbox (source: own representation)

9.2 The one-sided view (Part 2): Perceptual distortions

Two forms of perceptual distortion well-studied and frequently cited in social psychology follow here. Every reader will probably be familiar with these psychological mechanisms from their own experience – and though understandable, they are also tragic, because the person concerned, thinking that they perceive the situation clearly, is in reality already caught up in a view of things that leads ever deeper into escalation.

The fundamental attribution error

The first of the two mechanisms is the "fundamental perceptual error", frequently also called the "fundamental attribution error" (see Berry and Frederickson, 2015). Like personal attribution, it attempts to explain a complex event by using a simplified causal map. We can explain the cause as resulting either from our inherent characteristics or abilities or those of the other person (known as "dispositional attribution") or as resulting from external factors ("situational attribution"). The same situation can consequently be judged completely differently depending on the attribution. If the outcome is positive, our role determines the difference between "ability" and "luck" (Hamilton and Lordan, 2023). We tend to attribute success to ourselves (dispositional attribution, ability: "I made it happen because I am so accomplished!"), while we find external causes for the success of others (situational attribution, luck: "It was pure chance that he managed to pull that off!"). If we want to explain a negative outcome, we tend to switch attributions. In this case, our behaviour is seen as situational, inevitable in the circumstances: "I couldn't help it, I was forced to defend myself" while we describe the actions of others as dispositional: "That just shows his bad character!"

Thus, in conflict, the fundamental attribution error appears when we systematically disapprove of a person's behaviour. Then we tend to see their personality as the cause of their actions or intentions ("It's something bad in them!"), while we judge our behaviour in exactly the opposite way ("I had to do it!" or even "He made me do it, I would never have done it otherwise!"). Thus, we tend to justify our behaviour morally and contrast it with the supposedly negative intentions of the other person. Even if we behave destructively, we tend to shift the responsibility onto the other person – "I was forced to do it." The moral relief that people experience through this mechanism seems to be so important for their self-image that such explanations are invoked, for example even when a war is started,[52] in order to justify one's position.

Since the perspective of the other person is usually quite different and they will often assign the blame in exactly the reverse way, we can classify this form of faulty perception, just like the mechanisms mentioned in Section 9.1, as a ticket for the carousel of outrage and indignation. The conflict partners are led deeper and deeper into the conflict through their one-sided perceptions; both begin to "defend" themselves against the other.

The hostile perception error

While the first error of perception leads to the conflict, the second, known as the "hostile perception (or attributional) error", may then obstruct possible ways out. Once we become stuck in a conflict, we tend to stop giving the other party the benefit of the doubt. Everything that they do is *suspect*. Harmless or even constructive explanations for their behaviour are vehemently rejected ("You don't know him; he's just saying that!"). All our perceptions of the other party are overshadowed by distrust. They have – quite clearly – a negative motive, are doing this on purpose and deliberately want to make us angry.

This form of altered perception as a result of stress was initially observed in aggressive children (Dodge, 2006). In one study, teachers adopted three different facial expressions when approaching two groups of adolescents (friendly in the first, neutral in the second, cautious in the third). The first group comprised adolescents without reported problems; the second contained adolescents with a history of aggressive behaviour. The children in the first group reacted differently

---

52 While this chapter was being written in February 2022, Russia launched its attack on Ukraine, and in autumn/winter 2023, while working on the translation, the conflict between Palestine and Israel reached a new peak. The two situations present very difficult challenges in terms of avoiding falling into the trap of simplistic distinctions between good and evil in the face of open aggression (and not to be considered stupid or naive oneself in doing so). The arguments presented in Chapter 6 apply equally here: those who behave destructively must be held accountable for their behavior; however, we also need to recognise that the situation may have looked very different from the other party's perspective and that of the conflictual vicious circle in which they have become entangled. The use of open and large-scale state violence is the last stage of conflict escalation; there are no longer any means to resolve it because not even the law – indeed not even the UN as the highest authority – wields significant influence any longer. How can one escape such spirals of violence, which hold both sides captive, each in the grip of completely different experiences of reality? Both sides adhere to the "myth of redemptive violence" that Walter Wink found to be one of the most destructive stories in human society (2014, p. 50 ff.). We are confronted with complex questions here, to which no simple answer exists.

to each of the different facial expressions while those in the second group reacted similarly – aggressively – to all expressions. Thus, even a smile was met with something like, "What are you grinning at, do you think I'm funny or something?" Dodge concluded that in social situations dominated by distrust, it becomes difficult to adequately decode the intentions[53] of the other. Social role-taking and perspective-taking are limited and may lead to inaccurate attributions: the aggressive children could not "read" the cues of the teachers to identify their intentions. This mechanism is likely also active in conflict: "Those who are distrustful structure their perceptual situation in such a way that they attribute acts that might make an agent appear trustworthy not to that agent at all, but to other reasons (e.g. their own distrustful precautions)" (Luhmann, 1989, p. 49). The basic assumption is that others want to harm us – and that holds even if they behave constructively. Tragically, even friendly behaviour on the part of the other person is then interpreted negatively: "Now he's trying this underhanded trick!", "Does she think she can get away with stuff like that with me now? I'm not stupid!"

This makes possible ways out, in the form of a compromise or a gesture of reconciliation, more difficult. It is human nature that a variety of "inner voices" is found in each one of us, even in our so-called "opponents". It may sometimes be that one of the parties is in a more conciliatory mode – "Shouldn't we give reconciliation a chance?" However, if that person is then rebuffed just at the moment when they are making a small move towards reconciliation, they will tend to revert to escalation ("All right, I tried, but we can do it your way!"). The other person sees their mistrust as justified ("I knew he wasn't serious!") and the chance is lost. Thus, this way of perceiving social situations creates a context for self-fulfilling prophecies: a friendly offer is rejected brusquely or treated scornfully ("Oh, now you're trying to play nice with me? I don't buy it!"). When the other person reacts angrily, it is taken as proof that he had not been sincere all along. Thus, a spiral of "negative reciprocity" (Stierlin, 1979) is reinforced.

The following example comes from a conflict moderation between two brothers. One brother complained to the moderator, "Imagine, my brother had the gall to send me an invitation to his 60th birthday! It's obvious he's trying to mock me!" It was not easy for him to admit that it could possibly also have been a conciliatory gesture by his brother: "No, you don't know him, he's trying to trick me!" Only when the moderator asked whether his brother would have any chance of making him believe that he really had meant it honestly, did he think: "No, I probably wouldn't give him a chance." He

---

53 Therefore, he also spoke of a lack of "intention cue detection skills", i.e. the inability to correctly decode cues that indicate the other person's intention (Dodge, 2006).

realised that he was the one blocking a possibly conciliative step. In a later session, when his brother repeated the invitation, he no longer rejected it outright, but thanked him and promised to think it over.

To constructively influence a conflict dynamic, we recommend small gestures of appreciation and a demonstrable interest in improving the relationship, signalling a willingness to make the first move towards the other person (the one who takes this step is always the "stronger one", at least emotionally stronger). This gesture should be small (for example, bringing the other person a magazine that you know they like to read), given or shown almost "casually", not tied to any conditions, and without seeming an attempt at appeasement (Omer & von Schlippe, 2010; 2023). The likelihood of the hostile perception error must be taken into account: the chance of a rebuff is high and a friendly gesture is likely to be brusquely rejected, at least initially. The other person will want to show that they cannot be "manipulated". Here the person making the gesture needs strong nerves because the rejection of a well-meant offer is especially painful. If we know, however, that it is the hostile error of perception speaking through the other person, we can bear it more easily and react calmly. It is crucial – and this may be worth another entry in the conflict notebook – to react with equanimity to the rejection of such gestures: "Oh, you don't have to read the magazine. I just thought of you when I saw it at the railway station because I know that you were interested in that subject, so I bought it for you." Only thus can the hostile perception be constructively disrupted ("Hey, what ... there are no strings attached? Does she really mean it kindly?").

Fritz Glasl (2013) suggested a way in which this could be implemented in conflict moderation. I have previously taken it up and formulated it as an exercise (von Schlippe, 2018b) which I will detail again here. While the above-mentioned friendly gestures are suitable for so-called "one-party mediation", as they can be initiated unilaterally, this closely related exercise is also well suited to conflict work with two disputing parties and can help reduce mutual mistrust and reservations. It invites both sides to break the pattern of mistrust by making small gestures of goodwill. The typical pattern in conflicts is that one party is only willing to accommodate the other if certain conditions are met in advance. However, the other side interprets this as proof that the first party is not serious and demands that they make a concession first. Thus each party blocks the other's attempts to relieve the situation. During the exercise, both parties recognise how they can begin to overcome the pattern of conflict, step by step, by each making small concessions.

In mediation, talks are first held *separately*: each party is asked what both they and the other party could do to improve the atmosphere over a manageable period (about two weeks). Further questions are asked:
1. What small concessions would you like the other party to make? That is, what could they do to convince you of their good faith?
2. How should the other party make their offer clear to you? After one party has described how these offers could be communicated, the facilitator, as the third party, takes on the role of devil's advocate and raises objections: "How can you be sure that you're not being set up? If you accept this, aren't you revealing more than the other party?" etc.
3. What small concessions do you think the other party is expecting? Which ones could you offer on your own initiative?
4. How can you communicate this to the other side so that the risk of misunderstanding is as low as possible? Remember: The result may not necessarily be what you intended – often the starting point of a conflict lies in a misunderstanding. The accumulation of misunderstandings can be the real problem, or at least aggravate the real problem.
5. For which of your possible concessions could you waive guarantee conditions for the duration of the aforementioned two-week period if it is agreed instead that the effects of the offer will be reviewed after this period?
6. The facilitator ensures that, after a similar conversation with the other party, both parties put their offers on the table without discussing any other terms.

Preparing the offers separately introduces reciprocity, and the time limit of two weeks makes it easier for the parties to temporarily overlook the possible effects of their offers.

9.3 The one-sided view (Part 3): Protecting rigid viewpoints and the confirmation bias

Once people have formed an opinion about the other person, they tend to maintain it. Information that contradicts this opinion creates an unpleasant cognitive dissonance that we manage to avoid by paying less attention to it. However, the situation is quite different when it comes to information that confirms our beliefs and thus defends our point of view. This makes us feel justified in our position and good about ourselves. Thus, the search for information becomes self-reinforcing: everything that confirms our preferences is highlighted, while other information tends to be avoided, ignored or devalued ("Okay, you could see that action as positive – but that was an exception!"). This highly selective search for confirmatory information ("confirmation bias") represents another fatal mechanism on the carousel of outrage (Jonas, Schulz-Hardt, & Frey, 2001; Nickerson, 1998). Our thinking, which has already been strongly influenced by the other "filters" mentioned above, is now narrowed still further. The fatal element here, as in the hostile perception error, is that the potentially de-escalating behaviour of the other person is not perceived or is quickly reconfigured to fit the pre-conceived image we have of the other party: "Yes, he does that sometimes, but he doesn't mean it genuinely"; "I know her better, she's just trying to manipulate me with her fake friendliness". Once an opinion has been formed about another person, it is very difficult to relinquish it.

9.4 Groupthink: The equalisation of communication

The above-mentioned patterns of viewing reality through a one-sided distorted lens become even more pronounced in conflicts between different groups or even nations (Janis, 1991, 2011; Redlich & Rogmann, 2014). Disastrous dynamics can develop when thinking comes under the influence of peer pressure. This is often found within highly cohesive groups and teams where the desire for unanimity is greater than that for a realistic assessment of the possible alternatives. "It requires that members share a strong 'we-feeling' of solidarity and desire to maintain relationships within the group at all costs" (Janis, 1991, p. 237). When such group dynamics determine the decision-making, confirmation bias is often prevalent. The group members mutually reinforce each other's view of reality, but also watch each other to ensure that it is maintained. This pattern makes it increasingly difficult to consider and present possible constructive alternatives: anyone who does so is immediately ostracised and put under pressure ("How can you be so stupid as to believe that?"). Janis examined several cases of dramatically wrong decisions, such as the Challenger disaster of 1986 or the failed Bay of Pigs invasion after the rise of Fidel Castro. Here he examined audio records of the meetings of Kennedy's team. Kennedy had argued for the invasion and systematically favoured the advice of those advisers who agreed with him; opponents of the invasion were simply given less speaking time. This was confirmation bias in action. The Bay of Pigs invasion ended in failure and is considered Kennedy's worst decision (Janis, 1991).

9.5 Interim summary

"Fixed expectations create blind spots." This statement by the organisational researcher Karl Weick is to be found in his book on High-Reliability Organisations (HRO) (Weick & Sutcliffe, 2007). HROs are organisations in which errors can quickly lead to a high level of danger, such as nuclear power plants or aircraft carriers. These organisations must constantly and thoroughly scrutinise their decisions to determine the extent to which their perceptions are influenced by unchecked assumptions, errors in thinking or problematic group dynamics. One of the rules is that every employee – regardless of their position – should immediately act on and express any unease they may be feeling. A test procedure in a nuclear power plant is repeated in the case of any doubt; the take-off of an aircraft on an aircraft carrier is interrupted. Employees do not allow themselves to be deterred by the fact that the majority may not share their perceptions.

Groupthink is not only an external group phenomenon. In the case of conflict, the alternative voices of the "inner parliament" may also be silenced. It would be a good outcome for this chapter if we were to listen carefully to our alternative inner voices when they suggest that things could be different, that they are less fixed than we think. Similarly, it might be advisable to listen carefully to a perhaps lower-ranking member of the group who suggests an alternative viewpoint.

All the mechanisms discussed so far ensure that when we are on the carousel of outrage and indignation we become increasingly blind to our part in the conflict – and the carousel continues to turn.

10 Stupid, sick or evil: Demonisation

Figure 14: The demon (drawing and copyright: Björn von Schlippe)

> *Demonisation is an evolving attitude that begins with doubt, continues with suspicion, ends with certainty, and finally threatens to result in some form of violent action. Once a person gets into a mindset of demonisation, they look for clues and signs and hunt out the suspected hidden negative motives of the other. One must be vigilant and cautious even if – indeed, especially if – apparent attempts are being made at reassurance. Every detail, no matter how small, may become significant. (Omer, Alon, & von Schlippe, 2007, p. 25)*

The carousel has now gathered speed. Increasingly, our attitude towards the other person(s) is one characterised by suspicion and mistrust. The other person is moving in a logic that we cannot understand from our perspective (see the keyword polycontexturality in Chapter 4). Whenever we believe we have assessed the situation correctly, there appear to be only three possible explanations for the other person's remarks or actions: they are either stupid, sick or evil (occasionally we may be able to use the old excuse "Oh, you're drunk!", which is at least temporary). Stupid, sick, evil – explaining things in this way should sound familiar to everyone. Who has not shouted (or at least thought) "What are you doing?! Are you crazy?" at someone whose actions appeared incomprehensible? As long as this remains a superficial reaction and the other person responds with "Sorry, my mistake!" or something similar, there is no problem, but an entrenchment of this attitude towards the other person ("There's something wrong with him, he's lost his mind!") could also mean the conflict is escalating to a higher level. Chapters 8 and 15 describe how the conflict becomes more acute when the focus shifts from factual interests to personal attacks with insinuations of motives and character assassinations. The example of the two brothers mentioned in the last chapter shows this succinctly:

The two were joint owners of the paternal family business. A highly escalated conflict had built up over some years, and it was hardly possible to talk to them both in the same room together. In individual conversations it became clear how much they had become used to demonising each other. As both were educated, intelligent men, the labels "stupid" or "dumb" did not really fit, so instead they chose "sick" and "evil". One said to me, "You are a psychologist, so you will already have recognised that my brother is seriously mentally ill. I even know the diagnosis. But I don't want to do your work for you – you'll find it out yourself". In a subsequent conversation, the other brother commented to me, "My brother is a criminal, not 'like' a criminal, no, no! He is one! You need to know that and that is very important. Because like any good criminal, he has a story; it may even be that he believes in this story himself. But you have to be careful not to fall for it" (von Schlippe, 2014c, p. 128).

Transferred to another context and humorously exaggerated, this scenario is illustrated in Figure 15.

Figure 15: Demonisation (drawing and copyright: Björn von Schlippe)

Seen from a systems-theoretical point of view, the question of whether or not the other person may really be stupid, sick or – even worse – evil, cannot be answered because this approach does not ask how things "are" but, rather, how they are described: What kind of reality is evoked by what kind of description? In his book *Laws of Form,* the epistemologist George Spencer-Brown defines "drawing distinctions" as an elementary activity of all living things (Spencer-Brown, 1994). We make distinctions in order to understand the world around us. Something is distinguished from something else and only in this way does it become recognisable. From this perspective, the issue is not primarily the objective description of the thing but the *process of distinguishing and designating it by means of someone else* – the observer. "Everything that is said is said by an observer" (Maturana, cited in Pörksen, 2015, p. 4). We actively co-create the world we live in by making distinctions – and so, as cognisant beings in this world, we are also responsible for the distinctions we make.[54] Thus, the main question is not whether the distinctions are true or false but, rather, which distinctions we make in the process of building our personal view of reality. What aspects do they emphasise and what blind spots[55] do they create? For example, in deciding to use the term "evil", we create a distinction between good and evil. We label the parties involved with one term or another (the most popular format being "you – evil", "I – good"). Regardless of whether this is "right" ("right" versus "wrong" is another popular distinction!), from a systemic perspective we prefer to ask how helpful this good/bad distinction is, and what form of reality we create by using it.

The distinctions according to which we sort the world are often anything but harmless. Usually, we are unaware of the principles behind the distinctions we make; we believe we are making simple and innocent statements about reality, but once we begin to label each other or each other's behaviour, attitudes or emotions, something strange happens. Our distinctions and descriptions are

---

54 The way it is described here it may sound like a personal, conscious and individual process. But of course it is anything but: this process of labelling our world is a complex social co-creation in which no individual is completely free from the influence of the rest. And yet, each individual still has the freedom to become aware of the process that they are taking part in, to reflect on it, and ultimately to decide if they want to perpetuate it.
55 I am sorry that I have to deal with these important epistemological questions here in such an abbreviated way (see e.g. Maturana & Varela, 1987; Spencer-Brown, 1994; Kriz, Lück, & Heidbrink, 1987). Our mental and social world is created in complex processes of "observing", "differentiating" and "describing". Every observation is a distinction and as a description in language it becomes social reality. At the same time, every observation, every distinction and every description always means that something else is not observed, not distinguished, not described – blind spots are therefore unavoidable (see also Chapter 20).

not simply harmless depictions of reality but, rather, change the reality that they "describe". No one has become the person they are without having experienced multiple attributions and descriptions throughout their lives. We recognise ourselves through the mirror of others' descriptions (Tomasello, 2020). However, it is not only our own image that is conjured up in this descriptive mirror; the other person also "is" or "becomes" as we describe them.

By using demonising descriptions for people with whom we are caught in conflict, we contribute to the escalation. The Swiss writer Max Frisch addressed precisely this topic. Time and again in his novels, a person becomes who he is through the way he is described by others (especially, for example, in *Andorra*). In his diaries, Frisch writes, "To a certain extent, we are really the being that others see in us. Friend as well as enemy. And vice versa. We are also the authors of the others. We are responsible, secretly and inescapably, for the face they show us. We think we are the mirror and only seldom suspect how much the other person is in turn the mirror of our frozen projections. Our product, our victim" (Frisch, 1964, p. 33 f.).

Now, as the conflicting parties attack each other with demonising descriptions, the carousel is in full swing but the accompanying music is not fun. The stories told are based on demonising narratives that leave little room for manoeuvre. Every action of the other party is demonised and thinking is simplified to black-and-white distinctions such as good and evil. The way is now free for us to indulge in feelings such as anger, indignation and hatred, self-righteously and without ambivalence.

The actors are now caught in a process of mutual attribution. The communication pattern of demonising descriptions sets them in fundamental opposition to each other. Thus, as Max Frisch describes it, the other party now increasingly *becomes* the monstrous figure that they have been described as. Demonised zones (Glasl, 2013, p. 55 ff.) develop between the parties – neither takes responsibility for their actions and any damage caused is "the other's fault". The carousel is driven faster by "'collateral damage', when a disputant allows themselves to be driven to certain actions by strong emotions but does not feel responsible for their consequences, 'because, after all, they were not intentional!' – The reaction of the other party also follows this pattern and in turn triggers a mixture of intended and unintended effects" (Glasl, 2014a, p. 103 f.). Thus, bad things happen without anyone taking responsibility for their own actions: "He has only himself to blame for this!" (see Figure 16).

The topic of demonisation might lead to more fundamental themes. Don't they "really" exist, these narcissistic, mentally ill leaders that appear to pepper the world stage? Don't we worldwide have enough experience with such figures?

Figure 16: Demonised zones (drawing and copyright: Björn von Schlippe)

These questions (and I have asked them myself), if asked in this form can, of course, only be answered in the affirmative; everyone can list many examples from own experience or history right up until the present day. A perspective, however, which examines the process of demonisation sees the answers itself secondary. It looks instead at the *consequences of these descriptions,* that is, the kind of reality that emerges here. What is the contrast we create by describing ourselves as "healthy", "morally irreproachable" and (in contrast to our opponent) "fully in possession of our mental faculties"?[56] Any description inevitably comes with blind spots, and by using these kinds of descriptions we create huge blind spots!

In our conflict notebook, we could conclude this section with Wittgenstein's observation, "Everything that is described can also be described differently".

Thus, it is advisable to be careful and self-aware in making distinctions. Simple, black-and-white labels are usually of little use (except for making us feel, even if deceptively, that we are in the right). On the contrary, they are perhaps most harmful precisely when we need to talk to each other to find constructive ways of getting out of a conflict. Using "hard", immobilising descriptions will not soften harsh, frozen fronts.

---

56 Such labeling is of course very much "in the eye of the beholder" – like recently in a report in the news the USA were reported as describing Iran as an "Evil Empire", while Iran in turn was describing the USA as "Big Satan".

11 Watch out: Dangerous thoughts

Figure 17: Dangerous thoughts (drawing and copyright: Björn von Schlippe)

As if by magic, and largely without us even realising, the intensification of a conflict leads to changes in our thinking – and vice versa: changes in thinking also fuel conflict escalation. Emotion and cognition mutually fuel each other; intense feelings give rise to "dangerous thoughts" and we become stuck deeper and deeper in our own subjective worlds (the "Eigenwelten" that we mentioned in Section 3.5). In the heat of the conflict, the parties will often even be paradoxically similar in some aspects of their thinking. We have already mentioned Walter Wink's reflections on the "myth of redemptive violence" (2014) – a very dangerous belief system that is deeply embedded in our culture and often comes into play in escalated conflicts (without this belief no one would be able to lead wars that cost millions of lives!). On a more personal level, "It's him or me!" is a conviction that may be shared by both parties, or "Compromises are impossible – there can be only one winner and one loser!" or even, "There is only one right view of things, and that is mine. Whoever sees it differently can only be stupid, sick or evil!" (see Chapter 10), leading to, "If I give in now, I'll be totally destroyed, and the other person will have the final victory!" (Ciompi, 2005; Eidelson & Eidelson, 2003; Omer et al., 2007; Omer & von Schlippe, 2004; 2010).

What we rarely realise, especially if we are deeply embroiled in the conflict ourselves, is that both sides feel not only angry but often helpless as well (this sentence, by the way, might be a good one to include in the conflict notebook). They want the other side to behave differently at all costs – to give in to their demands – but they simply won't do so! The idea of being able to (or having to) control the other party has a flip side, and that is helplessness. The notions of control and helplessness can, in their "affect logic",[57] create the idea that a dispute can only be ended by the complete subjugation or even elimination of the other person. The conflict intensifies by any means. The danger lies in the irreversibility of the changes in thinking. Luc Ciompi, for example, speaks of psychological or spiritual "cancer" (2005, p. 214 f.) to emphasise the threatening nature of such thinking. Similarly extreme language is used by the Polish journalist Ryszard Kapuscinski, who describes fundamentalist thinking (the extreme intensification of this type of thinking) as a "plague" and notes, "A thinking that has been infected by this plague is self-contained, one-dimensional, monothematic; a thinking that always revolves around only one thing – the enemy. The thought of the enemy nourishes us, [and] allows us to exist. Therefore, the enemy is always present, always with us" (Kapuscinski, 1996, p. 324 f.).

There is a real danger in thinking this way. There seems to be only one way out of this cognitive trap – increasing escalation and redemptive violence. The following sections will outline a selection of these worlds of thought. They can be found on the individual level as well among groups of different sizes.

---

57 Sorry for these inconvenient words: It means, basically, that emotions and thinking are tightly connected and that thinking may dramatically change due to emotions: "fundamental affective states (or emotions, feelings, moods) are continuously and inseparably linked to all cognitive functioning (or 'thinking' and 'logic' in a broad sense) in such a way that they have essential organising and integrating effects on cognition" (Ciompi, 1997, p. 158; see also Ciompi & Tschacher, 2021, who speak of "embodied cognition").

11.1 The belief in the myth of power

> *"Powerful people [...] behave as if they had brain damage. In the literal sense. They are more impulsive, selfish, inconsiderate, arrogant, [and] narcissistic than average [...] They are more shameless and rarely display the very specific facial expression that makes humans unique in the animal kingdom. They do not blush. Power seems to act as a kind of anaesthetic that sets the subject apart from others"* (Bregman, 2020, p. 253).

To have power is to have a status that makes it possible to change the status of another person. This possibility, as indicated by the quotation above, profoundly changes a person and their thinking (Keltner, 2016). Seeing everything from the perspective of power has a direct effect on the course of conflicts. Underlying this structure of thinking is the idea of the possibility of power; the idea, in other words, that it might be possible to force another person, group or even nation to do exactly what *I* want. This clearly sets the tone: 'I want you to behave differently/to be different! And if *I* have not succeeded with my previous attempts to make you … [insert desired activity], then I will just have to intensify my efforts!' This is how wars start!

Gregory Bateson, who has studied power dynamics intensively, sees the "myth of power" as the core problem of humanity. He described it as an "epistemological error", even as imbecility and an epistemological sickness (1972, p. 487 f.). Power, he said, is an idea, a powerful idea, but one that endures only because we believe in it. For him, unilateral control is not possible: there can be no unilateral power, as "no part of such an internally interactive system can have unilateral control over the remainder or over any other part" (Bateson, 1972, p. 315). Every interaction is interpreted in categories of manipulation, tactics, strategy and control, and responded to accordingly. Moreover, a belief in the myth of power tends to corrupt those who have power (unfortunately we have only few "wise" men who are able to manage power). It is precisely because power is so successful that it is so dangerous. After all, "the slowly amassing effects of power" invite the abuse of power (Keltner, 2016, p. 8), similar are the famous words of Lord Acton: "Power tends to corrupt, and absolute power corrupts absolutely" "Anyone who desires a mythic abstraction must be insatiable" (Bateson, 1984, p. 272). The result is often destruction in the end, as history shows.

Conversely, even the strongest ruler is dependent on the cooperation of others (and must be constantly vigilant to retain it). "To assume that I possess power neglects [...] the systemic nature of things: If I am part of the system in which I move and try to have a causal effect, then I am always dependent on it and on how the other elements of the system act" (Nagel, 2021, p. 45). Power is a cultural phenomenon. The attempt to accumulate unlimited power is therefore "inherently tragic" because "everyone experiences defeat one day" (von Weizsäcker, 1977, p. 59).

The pathology of epistemology (Bateson, 1972, p. 486 ff.) lies in the delusion that it could be possible to be permanently stable, happy, safe and satisfied by using methods of control, manipulation, domination and – in the end – violence. It is a fallacy to believe that it would be possible, as part of a system, to completely control another part,[58] without this, in turn, having negative repercussions for oneself. Bateson considers our belief in power as a means of shaping relationships to be one of, if not the, greatest problem of human cognition (a "pathology of epistemology"), because the consequences are always destructive, and this is especially true in an era in which the possibilities for destructive escalation have greatly increased:[59] "When you have an effective enough technology so that one can really act upon your epistemological errors and can create havoc in the world in which you live, then the error is lethal" (Bateson, 1972, p. 493).

For clarity, Bateson does not claim that power is pure fiction. While it is indeed from the perspective of power theory a social construction (Anter, 2012), meaning that it cannot be attributed to anyone "as an inherent property or capability" (Luhmann, 2012, p. 23), at the same time, social constructions can solidify to bring real consequences:[60] people suffer and die from the power that others have seized. Conversely, the idea of power also "takes possession" of those who have it; once they have acquired power, they are in danger of becoming someone else without even being aware of it (as in the quotation at the beginning of the section). The belief in the myth of power – the idea that it is possible to reach a satisfactory state of interpersonal cooperation at some point by means of control, subjugation, suppression and ultimately violence – changes thinking and destroys relationships.

In many limited contexts, we are familiar with power differentiations that (more or less) function (organisations, military forces, schools, police forces)

---

[58] In the conflict notebook, a nice saying could be entered at this point: "The only person I can really change is myself – and even that is hard enough!"

[59] The two-sided nature of technological progress is succinctly reflected in a quotation from William Ury: "The use of guns did not just enhance one's ability to win the fight; it changed the very nature of fighting, destroying the sense of proportion [...] modern weapons change the very nature of what it means to fight. Weapons of mass destruction destroy all sense of proportion" (Ury, 2000, p. 88).

[60] The so-called "Thomas theorem" stated early on: "If men define situations as real, they are real in their consequences" (Thomas & Thomas, 1928, p. 571 f.).

but these examples involve simple task fulfilment – and even they depend on cooperation. The claim of an absolute exercise of power, however, destroys exactly this. This is what makes conflicts in the context of power and power differences so difficult, because some power strategies are not necessarily designed to find solutions but, rather, to unsettle and humiliate just for the "fun" of it (Ponschab, 2018).

Particularly in the context of personal relationships, people involved in power struggles – couples, families, teachers – experience the tragedy of believing in the myth of power. It is almost formulaic: the more we try to assert our own interests in a relationship by means of power, the more we lose the positive qualities of the relationship. They are replaced by the struggle for power – power displaces love. The power struggle is especially desperate when the fighting is about not losing rather than winning. Then the main question is how we can escape from an escalated power struggle – a "malignant clinch" (Stierlin, 1979) – without losing face.

11.2 Thinking in binary categories

A major problem in conflicts is the reduction of direct interpersonal contact. The opportunities to discuss, get to know and understand the other side's position become increasingly infrequent as the conflict deepens (contact is severed, diplomatic relations are broken off). The thinking thus becomes increasingly self-referential and disengaged from communication (in a group conflict there may still be communication, but the increasingly one-sided view of reality equally occurs here, on a group scale). Thinking becomes narrower, simpler and reduced to categories of either/or, black/white, good/evil. As described in Chapter 10, people often resort to simplistic distinctions to describe the situation. The map may be simple, but it leads us to a logic somewhat similar to that of the duel. In the rituals surrounding a duel, the opponents perversely cooperate. Paradoxically, they agree that honour can only be restored by the death of one of them. They know that they are moving in the same logic (the myth of redemptive violence), and thus can "cooperate" quite calmly, but with deadly hatred: "I leave the choice of weapons to you!" – "Very well! Where shall we meet?" What is happening here? The conflicting inner voices, which represent quite different views (Schulz von Thun, 2014) and thus also conciliatory ones, are unified (see "Groupthink" in Section 9.4). They can no longer be allowed because the parties are in an affect-logical state in which only total defeat or total victory is imaginable.

11.3 Our superiority and the otherness of others

A person's conviction that they are better than other people in important areas is combined with a feeling of being a special case and an entitlement to make special demands, to the extent that they come to see society's rules as irrelevant to them because they privilege their own thoughts, feelings and experiences. Groups can also share this idea. In this case, they are generally convinced of their moral superiority to another group, of being special in comparison, or even of belonging to a particularly select group (Eidelson & Eidelson, 2003, p. 184 f.).

The experience that accompanies this kind of thinking is that of being completely separate from the other person, the other being perceived as completely different from oneself. In a sense, they are not perceived as a real person at all, but rather as a kind of animal, demon or robot.[61] However when open contact is made, such assumptions can usually no longer be maintained: In a report on the "Holidays from War" campaign, where young people from hostile groups spent vacations together under professional moderation,[62] a Palestinian youth was quoted as saying about a moderated discussion group in which he took part: "When the Israeli girl started crying, I was completely amazed. I always thought Israelis had no feelings!" (quoted from memory).

The film "Merry Christmas" is set in 1914 during the First World War. It is based on the true story of how the soldiers of the enemy nations had been facing each other for months on the Western Front. On Christmas Eve, they agree an unofficial truce, communicating in signs and few words. The first Christmas carol begins, the other side responds with applause, and they begin to sing together. The soldiers leave their own trenches and meet in no-man's land, wishing each other a Merry Christmas and placing Christmas trees decorated with candles. The next day they can no longer shoot at each other. The officers on both sides work hard (and cruelly) to reintroduce the spirit of otherness in the soldiers, with only moderate success. The groups are torn apart; some are executed as ringleaders, others transferred to other sections or to the Eastern Front.

Those who move in the previously mentioned "demonised zones" (where parties act destructively without taking responsibility for their own actions) need asymmetry – the idea of the diabolical otherness of the other. This think-

---

[61] Racism is an extreme form of this way of thinking. Thus, in times of slavery, the severe physical punishment of slaves was justified by the belief that slaves did not feel pain in the same way that their masters did.

[62] For more on the project "Holidays from War: Dialogues across Borders", see https://wiedersprechen.org/ [last accessed 03.01.2024].

ing and corresponding rhetoric are not restricted to any one culture or form of conflict; fundamentalist and racist groups make use of them but in the fight against terrorism, for example, these overtones can also be found among democratic politicians or in the media.

At this point, I would like to mention two groups that impressed and moved me very much because they oppose this way of thinking with a particular strength. One is "Combatants for Peace",[63] a group of former fighters from Palestine and Israel who have come together as a result of their shared experience and realise that demonising the other is most certainly counterproductive to peace. Their film, *Disturbing the Peace,*[64] tells the story of how the group came into being despite initial concerns on both sides that the first contact might be a trap. The other group is the "Parents Circle"[65], an association of Israeli and Palestinian families who have one thing in common: they have all lost a family member, in most cases a child, due to terrorism or war-related fighting and have decided not to take the path of revenge but to reach out to each other instead. In the moving book *Apeirogon,* the story of two of these families – who had each experienced the loss of a daughter – is narrated by the fathers, Bassam and Rami (McCann, 2020). Instead of seeking revenge, they became close friends and decided to become politically active, telling their story to others and advocating for an end to the occupation and the violence. The Israeli father, Rami, tells how they first met and his account illustrates clearly both the destructive power of the idea of the other's otherness and the power that lies in letting it go:

"A bus stopped and several Palestinians got off. It was a shock. I knew there would be some, and yet I was stunned. Arabs? Going to the same meeting as Israelis? How was that possible? Thinking, feeling, breathing Palestinians? And then I saw this woman, all in black, in a traditional [...] dress with a headscarf – a woman whom in another place I might have mistaken for the mother of one of the murderers of my child. She [...] came slowly and gracefully towards me. And then I saw it, she was holding a photo of her daughter in front of her chest [...] I was thunderstruck: This woman had also lost her child. It sounds like a very simple insight, but it was not. I had been living in a kind of coffin and suddenly the lid popped open. Her pain was no different from my pain [...] The realisation was like a blow to the head that released me from my inner numbness."

---

63   https://cfpeace.org/ [last accessed 21.12.2023].
64   https://peacenews.com/disturbing-the-peace-new-film-reveals-hope-for-israel-palestine/ Retrieved 4/2/2022. Caution: not to be confused with the crime film of the same name.
65   https://www.theparentscircle.org/en/about_eng/ [Last accessed 02.04.2022].

A little later he adds:

"At that time I lacked the consciousness to admit it to myself [...] I was in my late forties, and for the first time in my life I saw Palestinians as human beings [...] as real people. I can't believe I'm saying this, it sounds totally wrong, but it was like a revelation – I recognized them as people who bore the same burden that I did, felt the same suffering" (McCann, 2021, p. 292 f., translated from the German version).

11.4 Basic distrust, conspiracies and secrecy

What we have already learned about the hostile perception error (Chapter 9) has its equivalent in thinking. It assumes the hostility and malicious intent of the other side. A realistic awareness that others do not always have positive intentions is a useful protective mechanism. However, if we fundamentally misinterpret their behaviour, this over-generalisation impairs our ability to distinguish people and situations in which trust, or at least cautious trust, may be appropriate (Eidelson & Eidelson, 2003, p. 187). In the logic of the conflict, everything our opponent does is seen as potentially directed against us. Therefore, in order to not be left behind, we must also conspire and secretly pursue our own plans in turn. The basic assumption is that nothing is as it seems. Even our opponent's positive behaviour is just a trick when seen through this mental lens (Chapter 9). Accordingly, we must also become covertly active and secretive in order to gain or maintain the upper hand, and also to maintain control within our own camp. Especially in group conflicts (for a detailed discussion of group conflicts, see Redlich & Rogmann, 2014), this kind of thinking can lead to a demand for social conformity within the group. The group largely seals itself off from external information. Thus, dangerous, self-contained worlds form in response to highly subjective "realities" that are by no means seen in the same way by external observers.

A suggestion from Niklas Luhmann could be entered into our conflict notebook at this point. He was well aware that blind trust can be dangerous: trust needs to be complemented with "auxiliary mechanisms of learning, symbolizing, controlling, sanctioning, and [...] force and attention" (Luhmann, 1989, p. 99). Yet he assumed that trust was "the strategy with the greatest reach. Steps towards building a culture of trust carry risk: the possibility of disappointment remains. At the same time, it is a special form of investment: "All trust begins with generosity. And it is very difficult to escape the charm of generously bestowed trust" (Sprenger, 2012, p. 135). Trust needs relationship, relationship needs trust. Then it has a chance of increasing social capital; the expected return is high but just as uncertain as on the stock exchange (von Schlippe, 2014d, p. 201).

11.5 The need for an immediate response

It is part of the conflictual mindset that the other party must never think for a moment that they have gained an advantage from their behaviour. Thus, according to this way of thinking, whatever our opponent does, we must respond as quickly as possible. In a tense conflict, our adrenaline-fuelled mindset demands that we strike back *immediately against the other side's action;* otherwise, we have already lost. It is precisely this logic that continues the escalation loop. As the escalation accelerates, so does the intensity of our reactions. Here it is easy to see how the conflict system increasingly narrows the actors' scope of behaviour. The only perceived option is to increase the escalation, and there is almost an obligation to do so: "There is no other way! I'm forced to act like this!" Like the concept of "no alternative", however, this "forced" is also a product of our thinking, resembling a "track laid out in language" (Wittgenstein, 2015, p. 166).

11.6 Sunk costs

The term "sunk costs" was originally used to describe a financial concept (the so-called "sunk-cost fallacy", see Haila-Fallah, 2017) that can also be applied to conflicts (von Kummer and von Schlippe, 2022).[66] If an investment already made has not yielded the desired result, people tend to continue investing time and money in the project in the hope that the earlier investment will ultimately pay off. Paradoxically, the more we have already invested in vain, the more we are likely to continue investing – a phenomenon reminiscent of gambling addiction: the stakes are increased by our irrational persistence.

We can see this thinking in personal conflicts. The maintenance of a conflict situation is also an "investment": we argue because we want the "right" outcome and, in doing so, we invest our emotions, thinking, and energy in producing written documents and money in consulting expensive lawyers. The more entrenched and chronic the conflict, the greater the obstacles to accepting that it cannot be resolved, and to letting go of the dispute or giving in.

---

66 The following remarks are largely based on our text.

Costs are termed "sunk" in bad investments if they are not amortised, cannot be reversed and cannot be influenced. The same is true in conflict – we cannot recover the time and energy we have invested in the conflict. The thinking error now lies in the fact that if we have already invested this much in the conflict, we want to win it, or at least not to lose face. All our commitment so far should not have been in vain! But this, again, fuels the vicious circle of escalation, the carousel.

Dealing with sunk costs is psychologically challenging: people find it hard to accept failure. The decision to write off failed investments – or an entrenched dispute – requires us to admit that we have made a loss-making wrong decision. Those who refuse to acknowledge this hold on to the belief that, somehow, they did the right thing and will still achieve a worthwhile result. This distortion of perception may protect their self-esteem, since no one likes to admit they are in the wrong, but the price may be high. Like throwing good money after bad, they waste precious time, energy and resources in keeping an entrenched, escalating conflict alive.

At this point, the following conflict notebook entry might be appropriate: Not every activity must be seen through to the end; sometimes it is better to abort the project and engage in damage limitation. It can be liberating to let go of the expectation that past investments will necessarily pay off. Winning freedom could be as simple as abandoning the conflict (which is not the same as giving in). The best way to avoid conflict is, of course, to recognise the signs of being drawn into an impending maelstrom early on and not to push the conflict so far that you can only think in terms of triumph or disaster.

12 Faster and faster: High-speed communication

Figure 18: "Always!" – "Never" (Drawing and copyright: Björn von Schlippe)

The previous chapters have explored events taking place on the mental level (perception, thinking) as well as those taking place at the level of social systems (communication). Since the last few chapters focused on the former, the next few will further explore the latter. Here, too, the options available to the actors narrow considerably as the carousel continues to spin: fixed patterns emerge in the actors' understandings and responses to one other. We have already encountered this in the hostile perception error described in Chapter 9. Once we have got on the carousel, it becomes increasingly difficult to stop it or even just to slow it down. The escalation of the conflict is self-perpetuating.

One form of conflict acceleration is what I like to call "high-speed communication" (or "calibrated loops", see Grimley, 2013). This is a communication pattern characterised by the speed with which one person reacts to the verbal or behavioural statements of the other. The parties involved believe they already know what the other is going to say (or what their behaviour means), so they do not fully pay attention. Of course, this is not always a bad thing: such abbreviated communication can be useful in certain situations, for example, when working together to mend something, a gesture being understood unquestioningly to mean, "Quick, hand me the screwdriver!"

When it comes to conflicts, however, the situation is different. We are probably all familiar with this pattern: You start to say a sentence, but after two or three words you are interrupted by the other person: "That's not true!"; "It wasn't like that at all!" or, (and this one is guaranteed to accelerate the carousel): "Rubbish! I'm really not listening to any more of this self-centred drivel!" The parties no longer ask questions; instead, they equate what they hear (or see in non-verbal cues) with what they already expect to hear, so they no longer need to check it because they already "know" (see Chapter 8). This blinds them to the subtleties of communication. They take it for granted that their assumptions about what the other person is saying are correct. Even if the other person's words do not quite match their expectations, they will make it match as they "know" what they "really" mean: "Well, you may say that, but what you really mean is this: ...". Their own perception is taken as truth and protected against any questioning.

The American family therapist Virginia Satir – who later co-founded NLP, Neuro-Linguistic Programming – together with her students identified the language characteristics typical of this pattern (Satir, 1988; see Plate, 2013 for an overview). They work together to create a pattern of high-speed communication, which is usually experienced by the participants as extremely distressing:

- *Mind reading:* Our own understanding is unquestioningly accepted as the truth. A potentially innocent question, such as "Has the order actually gone out to company X?" is unquestioningly understood as "I'm being checked up on again; I can't take it anymore!"[67] and answered accordingly in a biting manner. The other person may wonder what they have done wrong again. Sometimes it helps to realise that we have misinterpreted what was said.

In a conflict between a father and his adult son, the repeatedly violent reactions on both sides astonished me because they had very little to do with the content of what was said. After we had repeatedly gone over the dialogues ("What was said?" – "What was heard?"), the image of a "devaluation hearing aid" occurred to us – a device that both had in their ears, which "magnified" their thoughts and emotions and overlaid a

---

67 Peter Fuchs expresses it neatly: "We treat [...] thoughts as what they are not, namely communications" (Fuchs, 1993, p. 35).

negative meaning onto all that the other person said. The image of the "devaluation hearing aid" played an important role after that, not least because the term always triggered a smile in both of them.

- The assumption of *mind reading:* Without any explicit statements, one party behaves as if they had told the other what they want and expect ("She knows exactly what I want from her, but she doesn't do it!" or, even more problematically, "If she really loved me, she would ..."). We take it for granted that the other person knows what is going on inside ourselves – and if they do not behave accordingly, this is taken as a sign of unwillingness to find a solution. No clear statement or request or demand is made, but the other person is expected to behave as if it had been.
- *Avoiding taking a personal stand:* Instead of stating our needs or opinions, we use personal pronouns vaguely (we, they, someone) or resort to the passive voice ("It should be taken into consideration that ...").
- *A part of the message is taken for the whole:* We focus on just part of the communication while ignoring the rest. We tend to read the non-verbal clues and react, for example, only to facial expressions, such as a raised eyebrow, or the tone of voice without paying attention to the verbal content ("When he takes that tone with me, I already know I'm in the wrong again!").
- *Excessive generalisation:* The events of a specific situation are generalised[68] to all situations ("You see, it is always like this!"). Linguistically, universals are used, such as never, always, all. "'Always' never applies" is an oxymoron that always applies!

---

68 A small hint at this point: When things seem always to be "the same", find the differences! We tend to treat similar events as equal. A statement like, "You are exactly like my father!" ends every conversation. You put the other person in a fixed category, so to speak, and "know" what they are like. If you were to say instead, "You are very much like my father!" or "You sometimes remind me of my father!", new opportunities arise. You then become curious about the differences and ask in what ways the spouse or brother might also be different, and then you often realise that "You are similar to my father in such and such a way, but fortunately there are also many ways in which you are quite different from him!"
So, a little rule of thumb for the conflict notebook: avoid formulations like "exactly as" or "the same as" and replace them consistently by "similar". In our social and mental life, the word "the same" never really fits as nobody is "exactly the same" as anyone else (not even snowflakes are identical). Using "exactly the same as" in communication can be disastrous because you stop looking for differences and the conversation ends.

High-speed communication is, as the term implies, very rapid. Especially in couples therapy, it can be hard for a therapist to keep up with the partners' exchange of blows: it is like a tennis match, but often even faster! The antidote is, above all, to slow down and pay careful attention, allowing a new perception of the other party to emerge. This can be achieved through a controlled dialogue (an exercise that – as useful as it is – I always find a little tedious). The listener is only allowed to respond after they have paraphrased the speaker's statement in their own words. It is probably easier if there is a third person in the room who acts as a "professional translator" to slow things down. The little exercise presented in Section 3.6 on being aware of the "buttons" that easily trigger intense emotions in us may help here. If you recognise them, you could give the other party a "paradoxical tip" on exactly how they could get you to boiling point quickly. However, this is only recommended at low levels of escalation, or this little joke may come back to bite you!

An interesting methodological approach to dissolving high-speed communication loops in couples is a teaching practice from systemic therapy which I used for many years as a member of a therapeutic three-person team (Grabbe, Jürgens, & von Schlippe, 1998). We worked in such a way that one of us led the conversation, while the other two commented on the conversation as a reflecting team (RT; see Section 20.3 for details). In this systemic approach, the conversation is divided into different phases. Initially, one of the counsellors has a conversation with a couple (or family, team, or individual) in which they discuss various aspects of the problem. The other two watch the interview. After about 30–45 minutes the focus of attention changes (and this is repeated once or twice later in the session): now the two observers discuss the conversation that they have just followed while the others watch and listen. The session always ends with the client's commentary.

The basic idea is that it is much easier to pick up new perspectives in a relaxed way and to think them through in terms of our own situation when we are in listening mode. In a way, we observe ourselves by listening to how others observe us. Since we repeatedly experienced this high-speed communication in our work, especially in couples under stress, we considered a procedure that took the basic idea of the RT method and then modified it: we occasionally invited the people concerned to enter into a reflective position themselves (Drews et al., 2021). That is, in a couple's conversation, one of us led the interview with, for example, the husband, while the wife sat with the two observers and listened. In the reflection phase, she was then invited to reflect on her impressions with the co-observers, and the husband followed this reflecting conversation and commented on it briefly.

The two then switched and the husband now watched his partner being interviewed, without being allowed to intervene (but sharing his emotions and thoughts about the process in the reflecting session with the observing therapists). On several occasions, the couples experienced profound shock: it became clear at which points their intimate conversations in stressed everyday life were brought to a halt by a quick contradiction (which was now prevented by the change of the setting of the talk). Their understanding of what the other person felt and thought was frequently completely different from what they had "always known" and the feedback we received indicated that this approach had enabled them to get to know each other in a completely new way.

13 The memory of social systems: The transgenerational transmission of conflict

Figure 19: The power of stories (drawing and copyright: Björn von Schlippe)

One of the figures on the carousel looks a little different from the others and performs a particular function in keeping the carousel spinning for longer: it is the figure of stories and storytelling. The stories it tells are those of the deeply transformative experiences (both positive and negative) that we carry within ourselves. They are usually told only within our closest circles and can create strong ties between confidants (nothing brings people as close as a shared secret, see Imber-Black, 1999). Stories are a universal medium for remembering experiences and passing them on to others, sometimes over generations. The groups drawn into these story-bound webs can range in size from families, in "family memory" (Wetzel, 2022), to cultural memory structures involving ethnic groups or entire peoples (Assmann, 1988; Straub, 2010; 2019). Through storytelling, people locate their place in the world and ensure the propagation of their culture. Stories shape our image of ourselves, our relationship with ourselves and our "narrative identity" (Polkinghorne, 1988; Straub, 2005; 2019). Personal experiences flow into this image, as do the familial narrative worlds that frame it. Thus, stories as the "memory of social systems" (Luhmann, 1995; 2000) can also keep conflicts alive across generations, outliving the actors themselves, whether in family feuds, blood feuds, or wars (remember the term "hereditary enemy" from Chapter 6).

At the same time, stories are ephemeral. A story is not a photograph of an event, but only loosely connected to it as an active construction of consciousness. Stories are dynamic social events that convey a multitude of possible truths by being told again and again in the most diverse contexts: in the family, among friends, at school, in the workplace, and also by entering into non-verbal communication through the environment and body language. Particularly intense are those stories that are never overtly expressed but only hinted at, often through non-verbal signals, such as a groan or a grimace when war experiences are mentioned, for example (Mattes & Musfeld, 2005, p. 7, describe this as "symbolic performance").

The story – and this is important – is never an accurate, neutral observation of the events it describes. Rather, every story weaves events together to create something entirely new. In this way, the narrator is always also an author who conveys an explanation, a justification, and a certain understanding of the event relating to the narrative. This process begins in childhood: "It seems to be in the nature of the human mind that we look for explanations for everything that happens to us and to others [...]. The telling of a story is just one of many possible ways to arrange facts in a manageable way. It is the result of the mind's uninterrupted search for order, for a 'larger framework' in which an action can be embedded" (Stern, 2016, p. 137 f.).

And these processes, of course, do not emerge from nowhere: from childhood on, we learn which events are given significance, what our place is in life and within the family, and how we integrate into our culture and wider society: "Family members place the child in a specific location within the family and the family's history; they assign to it a culturally and individually pre-ordained place as a gendered being existing within a certain familial, national, and regional context. They convey familial belonging to the child. All this happens on the royal road of narrative embedding" (Boothe, 2009, p. 31).

We have already encountered the need for structure and order in the topics of expectations (Chapter 2) and causality (Chapter 5). That many of these organisational structures take the form of stories in the broadest sense is understandable: any experience, in order to be consciously remembered in such a way that it can be told to others and/or oneself, must be transformed into a story and, thus, becomes a narrative shaped by a particular author (Bruner, 1998, 1999). In this way, it then follows a logic of causal chains which are inherent to the story, a so-called plot: "Well, she said ... to me, and I was so angry that I said ... to her. But actually, there was no reason for them to then immediately ... well, that's going too far!"

Let us not, however, delve deeper into narrative theory at this point (for more details, see Jakob, Borcsa, Olthof, & von Schlippe, 2022; Polkinghorne, 1998; Straub, 2005, 2010, 2019). We want to focus on something else here, namely the role of conflict stories and their transmission in the carousel of indignation. A story has an effect – which may be positive or negative – even if it is only listened to it, because the feelings associated with it are shared socially through the telling. Listeners react with relief to the tale of a miraculous rescue; they are moved to hear how two lovers found each other; they laugh at a comical encounter, rejoice when fate punishes a villain and are outraged when they hear about injustice, humiliation and ongoing conflict.

A story is not only a way for the teller to structure their own world and experience. As communicative memory, stories also preserve the memories of a community, a family, a group or even entire peoples and nations (Gupta-Carlson, 2016; Straub, 2005; Welzer, 2010; Wetzel, 2022). So, stories don't simply "convey information", they also convey conflicts and interpretations of conflicts to future generations (von Schlippe, 2022b). Those stories are told to generate affective involvement; the listener is supposed to empathise and, in empathising, be convinced of the truth of the story. This is anything but trivial. Everyone knows what it is to hear the touching story of another person's trials and tribulations: it is hard to avoid being drawn in. Political groups and the media know exactly how to play on this: a statistic about unimaginable numbers of victims is less touching than the story of an individual, an interview with someone affected. Even if we know that we are being manipulated, it is difficult to remain entirely immune to it (in war, every party knows about this effect and uses it for propaganda purposes – you always find victims on both sides!).

Every one of us is born into a world of stories that our families have been sharing since long before our birth. We learn about our world through these stories. Imagine how difficult it will be for a child who is born in an area of severe conflict, with strongly biased stories passed down through generations! It is through these stories that the child learns about the world in which they live – they are told who the "good guys" are (us) and who the "bad guys" are (them). Conflicts are easily perpetuated when the narrators are not at peace with themselves, when painful experiences of injustice, loss or damage, or even of the death of loved ones have not been overcome. Such stories have a lasting effect on later generations because children naturally accept them uncritically and identify themselves wholeheartedly with the narrator to whom they are close: "Children who fantasise that they are their parents' saviour may perpetuate the unresolved conflict to a greater extreme than the parents themselves. Their indignation and their attachment give them a feeling of absolute moral justification. This creates a tragedy all of its own: someone who has experienced a serious grievance may, at some point, despite everything, approach the other party and try to bring the conflict to an end: 'Come on, let's bury the hatchet!' But this is only possible for our own grievances. It becomes exponentially more difficult in the case of old grievances involving those to whom a child is loyally connected from previous generations. Reconciliation would betray their loyalty to that person [...] The story has become set in stone, unchangeable. The conflict is continued by future generations to a point at which there can be no resolution. Massive transgenerational conflicts, or intergenerational feuds, may possibly be explained and reconstructed in this way" (von Schlippe, 2022b, p. 130 f.).

Second-hand memories of this kind can create loyalty bonds that are difficult to dissolve. Stories of injustices experienced may be told and passed on to grandchildren and great-grandchildren who did not even experience the events themselves, but who nevertheless feel the emotions associated with them. Wasn't Grandpa's partner always rejected by his siblings? Didn't his children suffer because of that? And why should you, even as a partner, cooperate with those who are responsible for "everything" that went wrong in the family?

The following example is taken in a slightly modified form from von Schlippe (2014c, p. 149):

A large entrepreneurial family had been very close for many years. The parents and the six siblings lived locally and near each other. They met constantly: "like one big family", the doors were always open and the children were "at home everywhere". But, as sometimes happens, at some point a quarrel arose. One of the siblings felt rejected and marginalised, especially because he had the impression that his wife was not really accepted by the others, so he built a fence around his house, thus disturbing the harmony of the big family. He was blamed for that, which only increased his feeling that he was not being treated well. Eventually, he and his family moved away from the town where all the founder's children lived with their families. His only daughter felt rejected by the extended family throughout her life. Although she had a significant share in the company, she took little active interest in its fortunes. Her son, also an only child, only knew his mother's side of the story. He was outraged by what had been done to his family. After he inherited the shares, he began to interfere vehemently in shareholders' meetings and attempted to intervene in all sorts of decisions: "No! Why should I agree to that now? You didn't make it easy for our family then!" Since more children had been born in the other families over the generations, he now had the largest single share. His voice carried some weight, and although he could not block the management of the company, he could certainly impair its smooth functioning. The only way he could exact revenge for the sins he believed had been committed against his family was by being a "spanner in the works". This was how he retaliated for the humiliation of earlier generations. To accommodate the others would have seemed to him like a betrayal of his family of origin.

Indignation caused by past misdeeds is passed onto future generations, thus refuelling the merry-go-round – this is how a conflict can last forever.

14 We've created a monster: The conflict as a parasitic social system

Figure 20: The octopus pulls the strings (drawing and copyright: Björn von Schlippe)

> "The destructive power of conflict does not lie in itself, still less in the damage to reputation, potential for action, affluence, or life that it inflicts on participants; it lies in a relationship with the system in which the conflict found an occasion and outlet – perhaps in a relationship with a neighbor, in a marriage or family, in a political party, at work, in international relations, etc. To this extent the metaphor of the parasitical existence of conflict is accurate; but the parasitism is typically not designed for symbiosis but tends to draw the host system into conflict to the extent that all attention and all resources are claimed for the conflict" (Luhmann, 1995, p. 390).

14.1 The conflict system

We have now moved a long way forward in the carousel of outrage and indignation (although since the carousel spins in a circle, any forward movement is of course an illusion). At this point, I would like to invite you to make another short excursion into systems theory. Let us return to Jürgen Kriz's graphic in the first chapter (see Figure 2). It illustrates how a system slowly emerges from repetitive processes and, after some time, begins to determine, even dominate, these processes.[69] In the previous chapters, it became clear how much we are influenced by archaic patterns as the carousel emerges. We react to conflictual events with "affect-logical reflexes" (automatised patterns in feeling-thinking), through which, without reflecting critically or even noticing, we allow the conflict system to emerge. This system then increasingly takes possession of us and forces us into its logic. The choice of actions we might take becomes narrower and narrower, and there is seemingly only one way forward – the one that leads to further escalation, unless we choose to consciously reflect on events, from above, so to speak, with a bird's eye view. But this requires swallowing one's pride (a German saying is: 'To jump over your own shadow'). We will discuss this further, particularly in Chapter 20.

Seeing conflict as a system can help us to let go of the idea that the conflict lies within another person and their mistakes and that it is in their power to end it (especially since ideas on whose responsibility this lies vary hugely, as mentioned). Alexander Kluge commented in an interview with Peter Neumann (2022) about the most extreme form of conflict, war: "In an antagonistic, plural world, you cannot decide. No one can. One can only negotiate or wage war. But it is precisely in war that one cannot decide. War is a demon that no one can control. In war, nothing can be decided. No one can win. Whoever wins, crashes [...] You must not even touch war, because it is infectious, like a virus."

It is important to step back from blaming the actors and to come to see them as prisoners of a conflict system which imposes its laws on them. This makes it easier to sidestep the question of guilt (although it does not mean not holding a person responsible for their actions). It is now clear that the conflict system that emerged from their interactions now dictates new kinds of interactions between the parties. It forces them into its very own logic, the logic of the carousel; the parties have, in a sense, created a "monster" that now holds them in its grip. In systems theory we talk of a "parasitic social system": "Conflicts are social systems, indeed, social systems formed out of occasions that are given in other systems but that do not assume the status of subsystems, and instead exist parasitically" (Luhmann, 1995, p. 389; Luhmann, 1996; see also Bonacker, 2008).

We need to take a closer look at what this means. A conflict needs an existing communication system in order to come into being. It enters into this system, so

---

69 In the language of synergetics (a variant of systems theory), an "order parameter" that develops over time, is said to "enslave" the dynamics of its constituent elements (Haken, 1992; Kriz, 2009, 2017a, 2017b; see also Figure 2 in the first chapter).

to speak, and "feeds" on the expectation structures. Before the conflict parasite entered, we might have a spectrum of positive, neutral and negative expectations of the other party, but as the parasite feeds, this range shrinks to only the negative part of the spectrum. The conflict destroys the normal, "appropriate" ways in which people respond to each other's behaviour: (Is it positive? – we smile. Is it neutral? – we respond equally neutrally. Is it negative? – we frown). The utterly negative expectations we now have led to further negative assumptions and reactions (is it positive? – unlikely. Is it neutral? – presumably not. Is it negative? – all hell breaks loose). Increasingly, attention and resources are claimed by the conflict for itself, while the actors are increasingly pulled into its internally consistent logic. Friend-foe relationships are formed – you are *either* for me *or* against me – in an extreme oversimplification of reality (Luhmann, 2013). With each interaction, the participants' freedom is reduced. Therefore, Luhmann also speaks of the "organisational power" of conflicts to create "highly integrated social systems" which increasingly restrict the behavioural range of those involved.

Conflicts do not arise from nowhere. They need the disavowal of an existing expectation structure or, to put it more simply, they need something to say no to. When two people first meet, there is no immediate conflict, unless they meet with preformed expectation structures ("Ah, you belong to the hostile ethnic group, so you are my enemy too!"). Without disappointed expectations, there is no conflict. Once a conflict is set in motion, however, it takes control and tends "to draw the host system into conflict to the extent that all attention and all resources are claimed for the conflict" (Luhmann, 1995, p. 390). Yes, the conflict takes on a life of its own and searches for people to perpetuate it. Thus, conflicts may sometimes last longer than the people currently involved in them.

In conflicts, therefore, there is essentially the danger of an erosion of the culture of everyday interactions – the daily common courtesies that we take for granted in our culture: returning the friendly greeting of a fellow hiker, handing the menu to the stranger at the next table who asks for it or holding the door open for the next person. In an escalated conflict, these common courtesies often disappear: A spouse's request for the salt is met with a "Go get it yourself!"; a colleague has the door slammed in his face; letters begin without "Dear" and end with no "kind regards". Once this stage has been reached it is very difficult to return from it.

I have on several occasions met teams where the situation had devolved to this extent. For example, one person would resolutely turn their head away whenever they encountered their hated colleague in the corridor. On another occasion, one worker took long detours to reach their office without passing the perpetually open office door of their opponent. One intervention that can bring a kind of healing shock (although it's by no means guaranteed!) is to ask the parties in the preliminary conversation whether the conflict has already reached this point. If they answer in the affirmative, you can say, "Then I am not able to work with you. It's probably too late and I am afraid there is no hope for you! However, if you decide you are willing to follow the basic rules of common courtesy, call me and I'll happily make an appointment with you!" This kind of reality check can help to shake the opponents out of their entrenched positions and bring them to a point where counselling will be much more productive if and when they decide to go ahead with it.

14.2 Demoralisation

The nature of the jointly generated "monster" means that both sides wear each other down while at the same time becoming trapped ever deeper in the conflict. Attempts to force the other party to behave as we would like them to regularly fail – are indeed fact bound to fail[70] – and eventually reach a point where those involved become helpless and demoralised: "It's hopeless!" As a facilitator, I can see clearly the grip that the conflict system has on the logic of the actors, but they are themselves fully convinced that the problem is just that the other party is incapable of reason. Suggestions become limited to extreme solutions, such as going to court or, better yet, how about hiring a hitman? Fortunately, this is an option rarely chosen on a domestic scale but in international conflicts violence and killing remain a popular "solution". We all know about the destructive consequences of this path, usually for all sides involved – as the rock singer Sting sang many years ago, "Nothing comes from violence, and nothing ever could."

We see here that one aspect of the conflict system is the idea that we can and must ensure that others behave as we wish them to. As this fails over and over again, we move further and further away from the option of re-entering a culture of cooperation, of "give and take". In fact, our insistence on bending the other person to our will only serves to escalate the conflict exponentially as the stakes become higher and each side becomes increasingly entrenched in their position (see Section 11.1 on the myth of power).

---

70 We've been through this before: the only person you can actively and purposefully change is yourself, as we all know – and that, as I have said, is hard enough. Even children can "only educate themselves" (Rotthaus, 2010). Of course, it is possible to support a person to change their ways, but only if they actively cooperate – and even then there is no guarantee.

Demoralisation is very serious. It weakens the motivation of those involved to participate in constructive solutions. It can, therefore, be helpful to repeatedly highlight any positive steps that have been taken, for example:
- That people are speaking to each other at all ("You have already taken the first big step. That is the most important one: to talk instead of letting the weapons talk!");
- That some common courtesy has been re-introduced ("I saw you greeting each other in a friendly manner/chatting in a relaxed manner at dinner ... I know of situations where the people involved can't even look at each other! It looks like there's hope here after all!);
- That progress has already been made in the form of small concessions on both sides (see Chapter 9);
- That, in the end, both sides may have a "third element" (see Chapter 21) on which they can agree (a value, a principle, a religious belief, a higher emotion such as love) which is more important than the dispute, for example, that the company (and the employees) should not suffer, that the children should be taken care of, that the cohesion of the family is most important or that loyalty to a grandfather comes before the conflict.

15 Not one step further: The horsemen of the apocalypse and the abyss

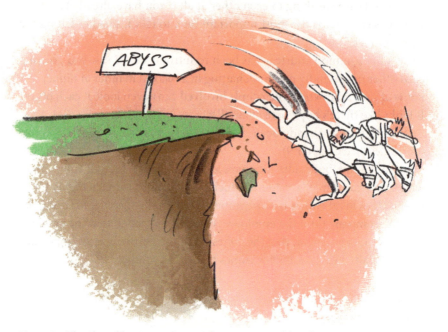

Figure 21: The Abyss (drawing and copyright: Björn von Schlippe)

> *"Hate is so much easier than reconciliation; no concessions or compromises are required. War offers the promise of victory and with it the tantalizing prospect of reparation for past humiliation [...] Rhetoric left reason far behind as the logic of war took command"* (Wright, 2016, p. 140 and p. 184).

15.1 The nine stages of escalation

In Chapter 8, while discussing the topic of self-esteem, we briefly touched on the ladder of conflict escalation developed by Fritz Glasl (Glasl, 2002; 2014b). The following picture shows the different steps going down the escalation ladder. Conflicts sometimes move quickly down the ladder, often more slowly. Sometimes they may become stuck at one stage for so long that they are no longer immediately recognisable as conflicts or become "cold conflicts" (Glasl, 2002; 2014a) in which the participants are resigned or afraid to explicitly engage in an open confrontation. This results in silent resignation, withdrawal and coldly formal interactions. However, the stalemate can also be quickly broken by some event: "That's enough!" In many cases, however, the steps are descended gradually, apace with the "increasing heat" produced by the hardening of viewpoints and increasingly polemical communication (see Figure 21). The last step, which is the ultimate destiny of any uncontrolled conflict (mutual destruction: "together into the abyss") is also the last stage of the carousel of indignation – a stage at which the carousel comes flying off its axis entirely.

Figure 22: Nine escalation stages according to Glasl (Source: von Schlippe & Rüsen, 2024; Drawing and copyright: Björn von Schlippe)

The nine individual stages will not be explicitly elaborated again here; there are some very good representations available (such as that by Glasl, 2002, 2014b; Ballreich & Glasl, 2011). Roughly the stages might be divided, first into an initial phase (approximately, Stages 1–3), in which a win-win outcome still seems possible – that both sides can still find their way out of the conflict with a satisfactory outcome. A decisive turning point is, as previously mentioned, the moment when the dynamic changes from a factual argument to personal attacks (about Stage 4). At this point the agitation in the conflict system increases significantly but, with some external help, the system can still be encouraged towards self-reflection. The following story is a perfect example of such a situation:

The team at the IFW (Institute for Family Therapy Weinheim) where I worked for several years had invited an American therapist to conduct a conversation with a family that was considered particularly difficult. The discussion was very turbulent; the arguments became louder and louder until the therapist suddenly lay down on the floor. Understandably, this abruptly stopped the discussion. Everyone looked at her: "What's going on now?" – "You know," said the therapist, "I wanted to see what's actually beneath the conflict. What is this actually about?" She sat back down, and the tone of the conversation changed significantly. An important question: What is it actually about? Until now, I have been rather reluctant to get down on the floor. But the effect is almost the same if you interrupt the conversation by saying, "I'd like to tell you a story!" (as we know from Chapter 13, people are always open to a story). In any case, whenever I told that story as the tension rose in a conversation, the result was often at least a small break in the escalation, usually in the form of laughter and thoughtfulness. This increased the likelihood that more would be said about whether the issues mattered more than the underlying feelings of grievance and injury.

This kind of intervention is appropriate if the affected parties are still to some degree responsive and willing to actively address the conflict, albeit with some support. It is in the later stages that the situation can become critical, for example, when defamatory attacks are made and the moral integrity of the other side is questioned (Stage 5). At this point, if not before, the conflict parties are usually no longer able to find their own way out of the escalation, especially when threats are added (Stage 6) and the level of fear rises. Conflict moderation by a third party at this point can help to sort the factual from the personal and support the sides in coming to an agreement. If this is not successful, however, another decisive threshold may be crossed: by Stage 7, one or both sides are set on harming the other – and it doesn't help any more to lie down on the floor! This can manifest as anything from a calculated humiliation, to a fistfight, to reporting the other party to the tax authorities or damaging an object cherished by the other. At Stage 8, these attacks become even more aggressive and aim to *destroy* the other by any means (nowadays rarely physically but in many other respects). Once this point is reached, Stage 9 is never far away, where each is ready to accept their own demise for the destruction of the opponent:

A successor from a family business told me that his uncle had dragged him through almost fifty lawsuits. The uncle had lost all but one of the court cases (which had ended in a settlement) so, in addition to the court costs, he also had to pay the legal fees of both sides. This battle probably consumed his entire fortune and must have caused untold emotional distress. The defendant also had to prepare for each trial, submit e-mails and documents, spending an uncountable amount of unreimbursed time, effort and manpower. William Ury, one of the fathers of the Harvard model of conflict moderation, quotes the French philosopher Voltaire, "I was never ruined but twice: once when I lost a lawsuit, and once when I won one" *(see also Ury, 2000, p. 87).*

In these last phases, traditional moderation is often no longer possible; rather, what is needed is "shuttle mediation", in which the mediator shuttles between the parties as a "go-between" in individual discussions. This can be "superior to face-to-face mediation precisely because of its result-oriented character and the reduced emotions" (Ponschab, 2014, p. 127).[71] An arbitral tribunal recognised by both sides can also help the parties to escape a messy situation. Sometimes, however, what is needed is simply "the UN", a third force that separates the parties. In all these cases, it is unlikely that personal relations will get back on track; it is more a question of arriving at a reasonably amicable separation with as little collateral damage as possible.

Sometimes the abyss is the last stage on the carousel: both may have lost their fortune, become ill from the conflict or even have died in its course. This is masterfully described in the 1989 film *The War of the Roses,* in which both ex-spouses, in trying to kill each other, are killed by the deliberate crash of a large chandelier. In the final scene, the hand that one of the two still reaches out to touch the other is brusquely pushed away – and both are dead.

Whatever the outcome, the parties (if they survive) usually remain firmly convinced that the other party is to blame for everything. The conflict monster, or parasite, can camouflage itself very well! The coldness that characterises interactions at this late stage can be difficult to bear:

---

71 Ponschab observes that this type of mediation is often also carried out as phone mediation, enabling people to be helped who would never have gone to a counselling practice on their own (2014, p. 127).

A long time after the end of conflict counselling, the daughter told me about one of the two brothers already mentioned in this book (her uncle and her father), with whom a colleague and I had engaged in a longer counselling process. She had gone to her uncle, who was also her godfather, and had implored him to be a little more compromising because she was worried about her father's health. The uncle had answered her: "So what if he dies, then he dies. I will not deviate one millimetre from my demands!" (von Schlippe & Quistorp, 2020)

15.2 The horsemen of the apocalypse

> *"Every marriage demands an effort to keep it on the right track; there is a constant tension within the emotional ecology of every couple between the forces that hold you together and those that can tear you apart. Even if you and your spouse have arrived at a stable pattern, you should be alert to the early warning signs that tell you if you are beginning to get shunted toward a dead end (Gottman, 1995, p. 69).*

The American couples' therapist John Gottman has described some typical communication features that announce the breakdown of a partnership. He calls these heralds "the horsemen of the apocalypse", a reference to the four figures who announce the Last Judgement and thus the end of the world in the Revelation of St John in the Bible (Gottman, 1993, 1994, 1995; Gottman & Levenson, 2000). Gottman found that the quality of couples' relationships and the likelihood of their long-term survival can be predicted reasonably accurately by looking at the communication patterns discernible in their verbal interactions. He made the striking claim that he could predict with 96 % accuracy whether a couple would break up within the next two years after having listened to an argument between them for only a few minutes. If the ratio of positive to negative statements is significantly lower than 5:1, the relationship becomes increasingly skewed; that is, one negative or critical gesture requires about five positive ones to balance it (the so-called "Gottman constant", see Figure 23).

The following "horsemen" will appear to varying degrees in tense conflict situations:
1. *Unrestrained criticism (you-sentences), accusations and blame*
   Here the other person is sharply criticised without consideration and accused without reason.

Figure 23: The "Gottman constant" (drawing and copyright: Björn von Schlippe)

2. *Defence and justification*
   Criticism is rejected, regardless of its truthfulness, and met with justifications and counter-criticisms; the party's own fault in the conflict is denied.
3. *Contempt*
   Any respect for each other has gone. Sarcasm and cynicism dominate the interactions both verbally and nonverbally, for example, eye-rolling, groaning at statements made by the other person, and so on. This "horseman" is described by Gottman as the most dangerous – paradoxically, it manifests itself in the context of a decrease in conflict intensity and volume: the partners become more and more indifferent to each other, which makes an imminent breakup of the relationship more likely.
4. *Blocking*
   Turning away from the other person; lost respect also shows itself physically (turning the back, leaving the room) in a total shutting down and freezing up, so that the other person talks as if to a wall.

In an own project, Christina Then-Bergh (now Strauß) and I examined the extent to which Gottman's analysis scheme might be applied in other system contexts, such as teams, organisations or larger family systems (Gottman's team focused exclusively on partnership conflicts). Since we had the opportunity to obtain the anonymised e-mail communications of various German entrepreneurial families who had been involved in severe conflicts to examine them for possible escalation patterns, we connected our initial question to the question of how the "horsemen of the apocalypse" change under the conditions of digital communication media (Then-Bergh and von Schlippe, 2020).

There are three particular dangers in digitalisation:
- First, there is the speed: conflictual communications that used to take several days to exchange by mail are now sent back and forth in a matter of minutes, allowing more rapid escalation.
- The next risk lies in the ability to vastly expand the circle of addressees: many people are easily drawn into the conflict via cc and bcc, and the "collective adrenaline rush" increases. If even a few of the recipients then feel compelled to join in and submit comments, the complexity grows exponentially.
- A third risk is the increase in possible misunderstandings and the resulting increase in conflict dynamics because the use of digital media reduces the information density of the message (Daft and Lengel, 1983, 1986). Different media are more or less suited to different purposes. The decisive factors include whether direct feedback is possible, whether natural language can be used and whether non-verbal signals can be received. If the purpose is purely to exchange information ("The meeting will take place on ... at ... o'clock in ..."), an e-mail or text message is sufficient. Personal messages are better not conveyed via digital media if relationships are strained.

Our study showed that in the digital interactions of families trapped in conflicts with medium to high escalation, similar patterns could be observed as in couple conflicts, but additional patterns emerged. In all, we found ten typical patterns (Bergh & von Schlippe, 2020, p. 279 ff., slightly abridged); you will find many connections to previous chapters of this book when the patterns are described:

1. *Devaluation, relentless criticism, reproaches*
   Here, the counterpart is attacked and their self-esteem threatened. This can happen through anything from a lack of greetings in a message to open verbal insults.
2. *Ultimatums and threats*
   Setting deadlines places the other party under pressure, and the threat of consequences increases this further. An example of this tactic would be "If you have not stated your position within the next 14 days, we will be forced to exclude you from the family meeting" or "If these tensions don't end by 30 November, all contact will be terminated."

3. *Irony and sarcasm*
   Here, something is claimed in an exaggerated manner that obviously does not correspond to the truth. These may be (deliberately) exaggerated misinterpretations of what has been said before, or general derisive statements.
4. *Distancing, formalisation of personal relationships*
   Withdrawing from personal contact and formalising communication are signs of distance. For example: addressing your brother as "Dear business partner" is roughly comparable to refusing a handshake in personal contact.
5. *One-sided attribution of cause, fundamental and hostile attribution errors*
   The insinuation that everything negative comes exclusively from the other side, while seeing no blame in oneself is characteristic here.
6. *Motive attribution and person-related blame attribution: analytic mode*
   Here, the assumption is that the other party simply has bad intentions. Pop psychology "diagnoses" are also not uncommon, such as: "You're obviously not able to take criticism at all."
7. *Expansion of the target group and formation of fronts*
   By enlarging the audience by copying others in on e-mails, an "us versus you" situation is created that isolates the person addressed. This is outwardly recognisable in the use of the "cc" function or sentences such as "The members of the family council are in agreement with me on the contents of this letter."
8. *Metaphorical shouting*
   The digital equivalent of shouting is expressed primarily through capitalisation, the repetition of punctuation marks (primarily exclamation marks or question marks) or the use of formatting options such as underlining and bold.
9. *Monetary hyperboles*
   Especially among entrepreneurial families, the exaggeration of money-related topics was noticeable in e-mail communication: "Of course, you people don't get out of bed for less than $10,000 a day!"
10. *Response speed*
    The change in the speed of the response allows conclusions to be drawn about the escalation level and the extent of the emotional arousal of the parties involved. For example, an increased frequency of e-mails within a short period indicates strong emotions, which tend to lead to faster escalation, as there is no time for reflection or questioning possible misinterpretations.

This provides an initial checklist that can be used to check the quality of e-mail and text message traffic for potential conflict escalators. Here, too, the following applies: "Prevention is the best intervention" (Ury, 2000, p. 139). It is always more sensible to tell the other person directly and openly if you feel offended by an e-mail than to shoot back with a public counter-attack. For this reason, we also offer ten suggestions for defusing conflictual digital messages in the aforementioned essay (Bergh & von Schlippe, 2020, p. 283, slightly modified):

1. *First of all, express your gratitude and let it stand, without immediately qualifying it with a 'but'.*
   Before replying, thank the other party for their message, e.g. "Thank you for your last mail. I think it's important that the dialogue between us continues ..."

2. *Pick up on the constructive, create good moments, and avoid sarcasm.*
   Emphasise positive aspects, such as the commitment shown; use appreciative language, such as: "I'm glad you care about our relationship ...", "I am impressed by your commitment ..." or "What I particularly liked about your e-mail was ...". Gottman, as mentioned, recommends a ratio of one negative to five positive interactions for a balanced relationship. If you are interested in de-escalating, therefore, always create some 'good moments' in personal contact. This may come in the form of a smile, a handshake or similar. In digital communication, this requires correspondingly explicit formulations: "I really am interested in improving our relationship ..."

3. *Address messages personally*
   The use of cc should be strongly limited, bcc avoided altogether. Conflicts should not be settled via messenger services in larger circles.

4. *Speaking non-judgementally*
   It is also helpful to speak directly, expressing concern without judgements on who is right or wrong, e.g. "Well, I understand that you ... I see it a little differently ..."; "That moved me ..."; "That struck me ...".

5. *Expression of regret*
   Express regret and correct misunderstandings, such as: "I understand now that what I wrote could be taken that way. I had meant it quite differently"; "I'm sorry!" (see also Section 18.6).

6. *The magic word "partly"*
   Agreeing in part with the other person can lead to them not feeling completely misunderstood; thus, the chance to resolve the conflict consensually is not destroyed from the outset by a complete rejection. An example of this might be, "I've thought about it again and I agree with you partly. I only ask you also to see that ..."

7. *Questions instead of diagnoses, anticipate your own errors*
   Put your interpretations of the other person's intentions in question form or

identify them as assumptions: "That was my impression ..."; "I'm not sure, is it perhaps primarily about this for you?"

8. *Avoid metaphorical shouting*
   Avoid all forms of ironic or stressing accentuation, and remain objective as such signals – especially digitally – can rarely be conveyed adequately and without misunderstanding.
9. *Send positive relationship signals*
   Express interest in a good (cooperative) relationship, compliment and make it clear that you want to work on resolving the conflict, e. g. "I would really like to improve our relationship"; "There are so many things I appreciate about you; it would be a shame if ..."
10. *Take your time*
    Managing the own feelings is central in conflicts. High levels of indignation can quickly lead to an escalating response. Often, especially in highly emotional situations, we misinterpret ambiguous signals, as is often the case in e-mail communication. Therefore, it is always a matter of letting our initial emotions subside and then writing a response in a reflective manner. "Forge the iron when it is cold!" (Omer & von Schlippe, 2004) – obviously "social irons" are forged better when they are cold.

This chapter ends the carousel. In a certain way, it is "always the same"; these are mechanisms that have evolved in our species over a long period and to which we fall prey if we do not consciously keep in mind that they are just that: mechanisms that evolution has provided us with in order to survive situations of low to medium complexity in which it was quickly a matter of life and death. In the present, in which we move to a much greater extent in symbolically structured and linguistically shaped environments, many of these mechanisms have become a burden because they prevent us from dealing with conflicts appropriately. They tempt us to move away from the facts and to abandon ourselves to them but the solution-patterns they offer us are just as archaic as the times in which they arose: 'It's either you or me!', 'There's no third option!' This leads to aggression until the destruction of the opponent – until war. The message of this book is to recognise that these outdated mechanisms prevent us from uniting, and from getting closer to a solution. Above all, they prevent us from understanding that we are much more similar than we think and that we always have a chance to handle our differences differently. Recognising this and acting on it, however, will not happen alone.

PART THREE: PATHWAYS THROUGH CONFLICT – THE POSSIBLE EXIT

Now that we have gone around so many times on the carousel, you may be feeling a little dizzy! You are probably ready to get off by now, so in this third part we will look at ways to help you do so, or at least to help slow the carousel down. I am not thinking primarily of professional conflict resolution. Therefore, as already mentioned in the "instruction manual" at the beginning of this book, I do not intend to offer detailed instructions for structured moderation or mediation procedures – there are already numerous highly recommended texts that cover this extensively, so I will give only brief impressions here. Tools of the trade and concrete instructions for consultation can be found, for example, in German in *Professionelle Konfliktlösung* (von Hertel, 2013), *Konfliktmanagement und Mediation in Organisationen* (Ballreich & Glasl, 2011), and *Systemisch-Lösungsorientierte Mediation und Konfliktklärung* (Lindemann, Mayer, & Osterfeld, 2018). In English, *Getting to Yes* on the excellent Harvard Concept (Fisher, Ury, & Patton, 2011; see also Fisher's 1997 book) is an obvious choice (with more than 15,000 citations). An extended version has recently been published in Germany (Fisher, Ury, & Patton, 2019), and Shapiro's 2016 elaboration on the Harvard model is also available in German, as well as *The dynamics of conflict resolution. A practitioner's guide* from Bernard Mayer (2000). *Contemporary conflict resolution* by Ramsbotham, Miall & Woodhouse (2011) also is worth a mention. The Austrian conflict researcher Fritz Glasl, well-known in the German-speaking community (see Glasl, 2013) brought out a practical book in English in 2002 entitled *Confronting Conflict. A First-aid Kit for Handling Conflict,* while *The Mediation Process* (Moore, 2003) offers a broad overview of mediation techniques.

The first part of this book was concerned with the "engine" of the carousel, describing conflict theoretically as a phenomenon in which a certain experience – namely outrage – combines with communicative processes to produce escalating vicious circles. The second part was devoted to the ride on the carousel itself and the many psychological mechanisms that develop "as if by themselves" in such dynamics.

The third part, which now follows, differs clearly from the preceding ones. It adopts a more personal stance, summarising much of my personal experiential knowledge, and is, therefore, written somewhat less scientifically. In addition to basic considerations of outrage and the management of conflicts, this part focuses on an aspect that is particularly important to me: consciousness-raising. The term was introduced by Harvey and Evans (1994) in relation to conflict in business families but I see it as valid in any conflictual situation. Those who understand the dynamics of conflict are no longer quite so unconsciously subject to their mechanisms. A transformed awareness can lead to a new set of actions, and small positive changes can support a more constructive development of conflict dynamics (think of the creation of "good moments" mentioned several times already). Accordingly, I focus less on methods or tools relating to outward action, preferring to remain true to my original intention in writing this book in focusing on "thinking tools" that can be used professionally as well as in the personal sphere, although the term "thinking tools" should of course not be taken to mean that recommendations for action cannot be derived from them.

Personally, the considerations presented below helped me to keep my own indignation (somewhat) in check and to maintain a channel of communication with those with whom I was in conflict. They also help me, when I am asked to engage in conflict conversations as a third party, to keep those conversations as cordial and productive as possible. It is not so much a matter of using as many techniques as possible but, rather, of helping to create a context where common ground and mutual understanding may emerge. Understanding[72] is for me the best way to increase the likelihood of constructive development. In escalated conflicts, this may in itself present a challenge, since one person can quickly perceive the other's understanding as an attack or partiality, although understanding does not necessarily mean agreeing or approving – or even absolving the other person of responsibility for their actions. Thus, I see friendly appreciation, empathy and authenticity (Rogers, 2012) as a basis for using various approaches and instruments in a relaxed way, as they are taught in counselling or therapy training. These approaches are not, however, the subject of this book, and it would be inappropriate to present them again here (for systemic practice see, for example, von Schlippe & Schweitzer, 2015; 2019).

---

72 In the broader sense of not just cognitive understanding but "standing in someone else's shoes".

16 The rehabilitation of outrage and indignation

A key task – as should by now be clear – is to resist giving in to feelings of outrage and indignation or at least to keep them within limits. They inevitably draw us into a dynamic for which we may be "designed by *nature*", but which at the same time can destroy the *culture of* our dealings with one another. The more we learn to see through the mechanisms that we inherited in the evolution of our species, the less we are subject to them. Indignation, and its particular drivers – blame, the attribution of often negative motives and the generally pejorative depiction of the "other" – create an almost inescapable gravitational pull from the moment they enter communication. However, outrage and indignation have come off rather badly in this book so far. It is probably time now to rehabilitate them, at least to a certain extent. There are indeed enough events in the world about which most of us would agree we *should* feel outrage (war-related destruction, genocide, handling of climate crisis etc., etc.). When we feel indignation, we feel that our most fundamental values have been violated. In displaying this indignation outwardly, we show that we are committed to fighting against injustice, that we will not tolerate it, and that we are determined to make our displeasure known (for example, by protesting about political decisions). Here too, the question remains as to how much we surrender to our internal dynamic of increasing outrage and indignation. As we know by now, there is another side to outrage. We are all familiar with what happens when public protest develops into a fury that turns into riots, and when the expression of outrage turns into violence. This second part of outrage and indignation is connected with the idea that any means are valid to make the other party behave in the way that we wish. They will probably react indignantly to our request – and, as we have seen several times already in this book – the escalation trap opens; the carousel begins to spin. The core question is therefore how outrage and indignation can be used constructively, perhaps even transformed, and how they can be expressed in such a way that positive results may be expected. Let us remember the first chapters: indignation arises when another person's actions run counter to our own value system, but indignation also means that we have not yet understood the other's horizon, the context in which they are acting. At this point, I would like to share my own experience of managing to transform my own indignation (slightly abridged from von Schlippe, 2020, p. 87).

Visiting an East German city, we are sitting in a taxi in a traffic jam. The taxi driver grumbles, "That building site has been here forever and they are getting nowhere, and it's supposed to take another seven years. What are they actually doing there?" He goes on – how the government can't get anything done, all the things they've messed up, the Berlin Airport fiasco, etc. I murmur agreement, these complex projects are indeed difficult to control …

Then a new tone enters the conversation, "And the Africans, they all come here! On holiday! At our expense!" – "Well, not exactly holiday – most of them are refugees," I interject. "No way, they just want to have a good time here, 400,000 come every year! And they're laughing up their sleeves!" I briefly feel the temptation to discuss facts, but engaging in this kind of debate feels pointless ("Fake press! Misinformation! You have no idea about the reality!"). I feel anger and indignation rising in me and consider whether I should demand that he stop and let us out there and then, except that we would be stuck with our suitcases in the middle of a congested street. Pragmatism wins out.

A dilemma – should I continue this unproductive discussion or make it clear that I cannot let these statements pass, which at the same time would allow him to become the victim ("See, it's come to the point that I'm not even allowed to say that anymore"). Fortunately, that is where I think of a third option: questions, and switch mode. "Listening to you, I figure you're probably going to vote for AfD,[73] right?" – "You can count on it!" – "What would they do differently?" – "Probably nothing, but they won't get into government anyway." – "So why give them your vote?" – "Well, somebody's got to do something different, it can't go on like this!" – "So, it's a protest vote?" – "Exactly!" – "What are you protesting about?" – "They just don't do anything for ordinary people. Nothing has changed in thirty years." I point out the renovated houses, and the well-maintained streets. "Yes, yes, but that's nothing. I was better off in the GDR[74] than I am today!" – "But you can travel now, can't you?" – "Yeah, well, who's going to pay for it? No, it was better back then!" We drive past the office of the Left Party, the "Linke". "Why don't you vote for them, they represent many of the positions that are important to you, don't they?" – "Them? They're part of the government here and they don't do

---

73 Alternative für Deutschland, a relatively new right-wing party in Germany, at the opposite end of the political spectrum from "Die Linke" ("The Left") mentioned later in this example.
74 The German Democratic Republic (GDR, also known as East Germany) whose communist government built a wall which separated East and West Germany until 1989.

anything. I used to vote for them!" – "But now you're disappointed in them?" – "Yes, they don't deliver anything they promise!"

I pause for thought. Disappointments have a lot to do with expectations and hopes. I think of Arlie Hochschild's study (2018), of the disappointment of Americans who had believed in the American Dream that "anyone can make it" (see Section 7.3) and compare it to the promise of "blooming landscapes" in the 1990s after the fall of the iron curtain in Germany. What expectations were raised then to have caused such disappointment today? I asked him, "What do you personally want?" – "For them to see what kind of situation I'm in: 68 years old and I've worked my whole life. My pension is 560 euros but my apartment costs 555 euros! How am I supposed to live on the 5 euros I have left? Why do you think I still have to drive a taxi?" – "Ah, I see, you feel like you've been left behind." – "What do you mean 'I'? That was a takeover back then, they ruined everything, our economy, our pride." I'm tempted to argue ("Do you know how weak the East German economy was back then …?!") but I hold back. "560 euros, that's really not much!" – "But you get social welfare then?" my wife interjects. "Social welfare?! That's no solution for someone who has worked all his life! You know, if I wouldn't get a tip from time to time, I would not be able to get by!" – Aha, I think, now I see where the conversation is going, but I am also calmer. We exchanged a few comments more and, in the end, I don't dislike the man that much anymore: I'm glad I stayed in the car. I give him a generous tip, and we laugh and say goodbye.

As the organisational researcher Henry Mintzberg so aptly puts it: "Start with an interesting question, not a fancy hypothesis. Hypotheses close me down, questions open me up" (Mintzberg, 2017, p. 184).

17 Who reigns when war reigns? Thoughts on the 'management' of conflicts

> *"Carter woke up on the eleventh day with the certainty that the situation was hopeless. He absolutely could not afford to stay away from the White House any longer. He asked the Egyptians and Israelis to prepare their final position documents and instructed his advisers to draft a speech he would deliver to Congress on Monday to explain why the summit had failed."*
>
> The quote is taken from *Thirteen Days in September* (Wright, 2016, p. 287, translated back from German by the author). It is a book about the Camp David negotiations between the US President Jimmy Carter and his counterparts Anwar al Sadat from Egypt and Menachem Begin from Israel. The plan was to successfully end the negotiations within five days; on the eleventh day, the mood was at an all-time low.

This report on the historic peace negotiations between Egypt and Israel, mediated by the United States, is an object lesson in how a chronic conflict which has long ruled how those involved interact with each other can also "reign" the dynamics of peace negotiations. The language gives it away: when conflict *reigns* then ... well conflict *reigns* and no conflict exerts more control than war.

In my view, conflicts cannot be "managed". The purpose – orientation of the term "management" implies the mechanistic handling of a phenomenon which – and this was an essential part of the first two parts of the book – has taken on a life of its own and tends now to take over the actors and align them with its conditions. To free ourselves from the spell of the carousel is laborious, requires self-awareness and is more comparable to a white-water rafting trip than a goal-oriented process. "Management" – a behind which a "myth of absolute control" can be assumed (Gehmann, 2016) – is thus associated with a promise that will rarely be fully realised. Therefore, I am also careful with the terms "goal" and "solution" (terms which are bandied about too carelessly, in my opinion). I have rarely experienced "Hollywood endings" to conflict consultations. Much has already been gained when the carousel is slowed down, when the parties involved demonise each other to a lesser extent (even if they usually continue to think the other is the real cause of the problem) even when they are relieved that some of the factual issues have been resolved and when they can get along with each other again to some extent. A greater distance often remains. When profound reconciliation occurs (and I have also experienced this), it is a great gift. As a highly committed facilitator, despite my professional role, I find myself again and again experiencing a mixture of perplexity and awe when confronted with the impact that a history of deep injuries and loss has on each individual, and when I see the deep-seated resentments that make the parties so remote from each other. Sometimes I shy away from the hatred that those involved feel towards each other and the fear and mistrust that dominate their interactions despite, from my perspective, the other party's demonstrably good intentions.

Lawrence Wright's excellent book, quoted at the beginning of this chapter, describes impressively how much one is exposed to all these forces in the moderation process and how little conscious control is possible. Although he describes a conflict between two nations that had lasted for decades, the feelings in highly escalated and chronic permanent conflicts in other contexts are comparable. In his book, Wright shows how the Camp David negotiations were scheduled to last for five days but had to be repeatedly extended. Under the committed moderation of the US president, whose political fate was also at stake here, the presidents of Israel and Egypt fought for their positions, in some cases even opposing members of their own delegation. The interests that had brought them to these positions were clear, "Some words were […] so charged that they could not be used without provoking strong reactions" (Wright, 2016, p. 299 f.). Roger Fisher, the creator of the Harvard model (Fisher, 1989, 1997; Fisher, Ury, & Patton, 2011), was also involved (Ponschab, 2015, p. 272). Yet time and time again, the crisis point was reached; time and time again, the mood fluctuated between hope and despair, as the quotation above exemplifies. More than once, the talks were close to being abandoned; more than once, the helicopters were ordered for the departure of one or another. Small coincidences, luck, personal relationships and friendships, fear of embarrassment and, of course, persuasion and negotiating skills ensured, time and time again, that some progress was made. Even on the last day, the hard-won compromise (mainly concerning Jewish settlements in the Sinai, the status of Jerusalem and the rights of the Palestinians) was on perilously shaky ground, and the meeting was a hair's breadth from collapsing without success. Each side had to lower their expectations, and in the end, everyone was disappointed, but a minimal consensus had been found – albeit at the price of not resolving the Palestinian issue or the settlements on the West Bank.

Now the renunciation of the term "management" and the attitude associated with it does not mean that nothing can be done. On the contrary, Jimmy Carter invested all the commitment his personality and his official position could muster into it: he talked to the individual representatives of the delegations, made his own proposals and showed his annoyance and his anger very clearly when once again an agreement which had been within reach burst like a soap bubble because of one party's objection. Staying with the white-water rafting metaphor, even Carter, an experienced "boatsman", was overwhelmed by the force of some of the waves and hit his head hard on the rocks several times; only at the very end did it become clear that the ride had been worth it. For me, this is also the difference between therapy and conflict work: as a consultant, I look at contentious issues together with the disputants and consider possible solutions. Although I am generally considered to be calm by nature, I have also been known to bang my fist on the table in conflict counselling sessions when I felt that, just as we were approaching our goal, one of the parties was trying to start the carousel up again.[75] I was relieved to read that Carter had, apparently, felt the same way on several occasions, frustrated by the obstinacy of the conflict parties: "It was heartbreaking to see how insignificant the differences really were when measured against the lasting benefits of peace" (Wright, 2016, p. 280). Eventually, Israel agreed to give up the Jewish settlements in the Sinai which had been disputed until the very end. A peace treaty was reached between Israel and Egypt, the terms of which have not been violated since 1979 (Wright, 2016, p. 356).

---

75 At least once, after the initial shock of my emotional reaction, my smartwatch unexpectedly de-stressed the situation by saying very audibly, "You seem to have fallen. Do you need help?" Everyone dissolved into laughter; sometimes coincidence comes at the right time!

18 "Consciousness raising", becoming aware of automatic mechanisms and self-work

> *"In a word, your perceptual machinery, the way you perceive, is governed by a system of presuppositions that I call your epistemology: a whole philosophy deep inside your mind but beyond your consciousness"* (Bateson & Bateson, 2005, p. 136).

Most of the patterns described in the carousel section (Part 2) of this book are part of the equipment acquired through evolution to enable us to survive in environments that were both manageable and, at the same time, full of life-threatening dangers. Our perception and our reaction patterns enabled us – and still enable us – to quickly assess situations emotionally and act just as quickly according to our emotions. However, the basic conditions of human life have changed dramatically in the meantime. Today, we live in largely artificially created environments; we have constant access to information from every corner of the globe (although whether that information is accurate is another question); we can always be reached via telephone and other media, and most of us do not have to constantly fear for our lives. Many of our ingrained conflictual survival patterns, therefore, become a problem for us if we surrender to them unconsciously and without reflection.

The central point is to become aware of these mechanisms in the sense of the initial quote. I have already mentioned a term that I have come across in this context – "consciousness raising", that is, working on one's own consciousness in conflict (Harvey & Evans, 1994; see also von Schlippe & Frank, 2017). It is a mistake to believe that anyone sitting on the carousel could (or even should) have a full overview of all aspects involved in any carousel of outrage and indignation (see Chapter 17). It is the unreflecting and automatic behaviour of each of the parties involved that drives the escalation. Therefore, I consider *self-work* to be a central task in working on conflict. If we learn to be aware, to become an observer of ourselves, and to deal with our own agitation in ways that do not perpetuate the escalation, then we are on the right path. The practice of self-work raises numerous possibilities for breaking the compulsive escalation within a conflict and for increasing the likelihood of more constructive encounters.

18.1 The art of the unexpected response

> *"An interruption of the vicious circle becomes possible if a provocation is not followed by the hostile reaction expected but instead by an unexpectedly level-headed response! This is not merely the naive wishful thinking of theorists far removed from reality but has proven itself in escalated international conflicts"* (Gareis, Kulessa, Hasse, Glasl, & Brzoska, 2014, p. 271).

In trying to change a parasitic communication system, we have to withstand considerable resistance. We can begin to prepare the way for the desired change by asking ourselves what reaction we expect to any of our actions. Conflicts are, after all, characterised by negative expectation structures. By not meeting these expectations, or even doing the opposite, we introduce an element of surprise. The saying from the Bible about 'turning the other cheek' is not an invitation to masochism, but an invitation to do the unexpected! In this way, we give the "butterfly effect" a chance to take the conflict in a new (and hopefully positive) direction just by doing something different.

In this respect, it is key to reflect on our own indignation, or indeed to perceive it in the first place. The more fully we become aware of it, the sooner we can learn to resist its invitation to be drawn into automatic reactions; to not act out of immediate indignation, but to slow down and reconsider. Adrenalin is never a good adviser. The great challenge of consciousness and awareness lies in resisting the pull of escalation. This is the hardest step, since the opportunities to become "sucked in" are numerous: the little taunts, the outright nastiness or the "totally unfair" attempts to exert dominance. Our self-esteem takes a blow, tempting us to fall into a "call-to-arms-reflex" (Glasl) and to strike back blindly.

Consciousness begins with recognising such mechanisms for what they are. Then we are no longer completely at their mercy and can interact with "guarded friendliness" (Ponschab, 2018, p. 257) or simply make ourselves unpredictable (as ironically exaggerated in Figure 24). To achieve this, it can help to imagine that you are an observer of the scene: in your imagination, get up, stand next to yourself[76] and simply observe what is happening. Notice how, by doing so,

---

[76] In coaching, you can play this out: get up from your chair, which is facing the "opponent" (who is imagined and not physically present), and stand next to them in order to view the

your picture of the conflict process changes. Instead of indignantly thinking – or even saying – how "stupid, evil, unbearable" the other party is, you instead become aware of which of your "buttons" they are skilfully pushing,[77] knowing exactly how "best" to upset you.

It is important to stop these loops, because your excitement and agitation symbolically feed the other party (as well as the conflict parasite, your "monster"). If, however, you step out of the scene inwardly (to be "beside yourself" in a positive sense) in order to observe yourself in the conflict situation, you open the door to new questions such as:
- What is happening here right now?
- What might the other person want to achieve by making that statement and/or action? What kind of reaction are they expecting from me? What do they expect me to do – or not to do – now?
- Which of my buttons are being pushed right now and what is happening within me as a result?
- Are we on a good path right now? Do I want to carry on along it?
- What do I need now to stand firm and remain capable of acting prudently? Perhaps we need an interruption, a break (see Section 18.2)?

These are questions that, depending on the situation, can be asked openly, but it may be even more productive to explore what an unexpected reaction might look like. Simply continuing along the well-worn path of our usual behaviour maintains the logic of the conflict. Sometimes it is enough to follow the time-honoured prompt of solution-focused therapy: "Do something different!" (reminiscent of a quote frequently attributed to Albert Einstein: "The definition of insanity is doing the same thing over and over again and expecting different results", see also Groth, 2017, p. 75). The focus here should not be on shaking the other person up (although that might be a side-effect, for better or for worse!), but on adopting a curious and experimental stance[78] that may surprise your-

---

scene from a different perspective with a view of both chairs, asking yourself the questions listed above. Having played this out makes it easier to do it mentally in a real-life situation, or even to dare to stand up and change the perspective there too.

77 In the sense of the small exercise in Section 3.6
78 Once you start doing this, it can even be fun in everyday life. The invitation to "do something different" can apply to many areas of life that would benefit from being shaken out of their routine. Which foot do you usually get out of bed first with? On which side of the bed do you/your partner sleep and have you ever switched? Have you ever spent a night outdoors? When buying food in the deli, how about copying the selection that the person before you bought instead of taking your usual favourite assortment? Or try something similar when buying clothes. Have you ever been to a carnival, a casino, a horse race, the opera, a classical/punk

self even more: what actually happens in terms of possible new communicative connections when I break out of my habitual behavioural patterns? (von Schlippe, 2014c, p. 162).

Figure 24: "Make yourself unpredictable" (drawing and copyright: Björn von Schlippe)

Clearly, one side deciding to step out of the vicious circle does not automatically mean that the other side is also ready to do so. On the contrary, we must expect that the parasite – the system of negative expectations – will try to re-establish itself. The other side will perhaps – initially even more than before – seek confrontation, which has become such a part of everyday life. Remember: your outrage is "food" for the parasite, and it won't like you withholding its next meal! Changing escalation habits takes time, but the following are a few ideas that help to resist the temptation to react in an escalating manner:
- Slowing down is often a better alternative than immediately striking back. At the point where you would usually react with rage and aggression, try instead to calm your nervous system down a little. Some simple "self-care" steps can help with this, for example: taking deep breaths, especially exhaling (Ponschab, 2018, p. 260), or counting to 100 (sometimes probably rather to

---

or rock concert? Have you ever stayed the night in a tree house? Have you ever gone to a billiards or darts world championship? Have you ever played 'roulette' by going to the cinema or theatre and blindly buying a ticket for the film or play without knowing what it's about?

1000 or more!) before reacting (provided you want to change something, of course). If your response then turns out to be a little weaker than expected, you're on the right track.
- For parents, one tip for moments like these is to say the following sentence silently, like a mantra in meditation: *"I won't let myself get involved!"* This way the mind is temporarily occupied with something other than being outraged.
- Sometimes it is certainly appropriate to draw a line calmly without, for example, violating the other person's boundary through a counter-insult: "This is too much for me now!" or "I can see we're not going to be able to come to an agreement at this moment so I would like to drop the matter for now and come back to it later."
- An unexpected response to provocation, rather than rushing into an angry response, might be to enquire (with genuine interest!),[79] "What do you mean by that exactly?", "Can you elaborate on that a bit more?", "What do you mean by 'never'?" or similar (see Thiele, 2018, p. 105, where other "repartee techniques" are also listed).
- Indirect "questions with constructive presuppositions" (von Hertel, 2013, p. 207 f.), which convey the expectation of a plausible intention behind the provocation, could be particularly useful here. It is best to present these questions as statement sentences that are less demanding than a direct question: "I don't think I've quite understood yet why this is important to you", "I'm wondering what exactly you think should be changed", or "I wonder what you would answer right now if you were me."
- It won't always succeed, but it would be a significant step away from the "automatic" reaction pattern if a reframing could be found so that the parties are starting from a constructive place. This reframing could be expressed verbally, "Of course, it's not easy right now, but I must say that I'm impressed by your engagement and your commitment to change!" Or, the reframing could simply be in the way you *think* about a situation: personal hostility could be seen instead as a (somewhat clumsy) attempt by the other party to protect their threatened sense of self-esteem. This kind of reinterpretation may help you to stay more relaxed in the situation.
- As previously mentioned, the little word "partly" can be a magic word. It does not fulfil the expectation of escalation but at the same time is not a total concession. There are many nuances between black and white, and a sense

---

79 Generally, however, "why questions" should be avoided; as a rule, they do not lead anywhere (von Hertel, 2013, p. 205).

of differentiation can be introduced here: "I partly agree with you"; "I can partly understand what you mean".

Figure 25: Partly (drawing and copyright: Björn von Schlippe)

– Finally, it can help to engage in the kind of self-talk that begins, "How interesting ..." (Groth, 2017, p. 13), inviting curiosity. Indignation is linked to judgement ("How shameless!"), while curiosity invites us, rather, to see the situation as a difficult puzzle. Obviously, we have not yet grasped what makes the other person tick: "Those who understand quickly may not have understood at all" (Groth, 2017, p. 13). Curiosity leads us into observation mode: "How interesting that ..."

18.2 "The First-Aid break"

No matter how well we know the value of remaining calm in the face of attacks and of not getting involved in emotional games, in the heat of the moment we may simply forget our good resolutions. The ferocity of the attack may feel unbearable – we feel as if we could explode, and the longer we manage to keep a lid on our reaction, the bigger the bang when we finally let fly. Here, a useful tactic may be to call for a time out to prevent escalation. It is important to introduce this break well, because not every interruption has a de-escalating effect. To remain silent in a huff ("I'm not saying anything anymore now!") or to get up and slam the door in a rage (perhaps having delivered a parting insult over our shoulder on the way) unnecessarily increases the tension and negative feelings on both sides.

If, on the other hand, we introduce an interruption by announcing that we will come back to the topic when everyone is calmer, we are following the motto "Forge the iron when it is cold" (Omer and von Schlippe, 2004). "Social iron" (unlike real iron) is, as previously mentioned, "forged better when cold". A constructive interruption is one where we make clear that we are "leaving, in order to stay" (a handy mnemonic for the conflict notebook, by the way!). "I realise that I am very stressed right now. I might say or do something that I wouldn't feel good about later. I need some time out right now, but I'll come back to it later" or: "No, I don't like it and I don't agree with it, but I'll think about it. I am too unsettled now to figure it out calmly!" Clear markers like these can help to interrupt an escalation but keep the door open to return to the issue later when in a better frame of mind.

If both sides (e.g. in a couple) see the sense of such a break but have difficulty regulating their own distress in certain situations, it can be helpful in a longer-lasting conflict moderation to find a "safe word" to create the break. For example, the term "time out" could be a signal for both parties to immediately distance themselves from each other and avoid any interaction for at least an hour to prevent themselves from doing or saying things that they may regret later.

18.3 "Neither too many nor too few words!"

When we are agitated, we tend to use too many words, to repeat ourselves, to over-explain and to demand. Usually, all this is not done with calm and friendly congeniality. Excessive explanations, however, tend to exacerbate conflict dynamics (Simon, 2012, p. 35). The more words we use, the more we repeat our position and (even if we are making such eminently sensible suggestions as "I've already told you umpteen times that you should read von Schlippe's conflict book!"), the less the other person will pay attention to what we say. Adolescents tend to react extremely negatively to "parental nagging" (see Omer & von Schlippe, 2023). At best, the other party will just stop listening; most of the time, however, both parties will work themselves into an incoherent lather. Simon recommends that if explanations cannot be avoided, they should at least be structured to ascribe sincere motives to each party ("I'm sure that Beth only wanted to prevent John from getting hurt and John just wanted to prove that he could act independently" etc.) in order to avoid arguments over who is correct (Simon, 2012, p. 35).

The idea here is not to cut off communication, but just the self-perpetuating cycle of explanations and counter-explanations, and the corresponding cycle of misunderstandings and counter-misunderstandings. This avoidance of "explanatory loops" is not the same as the rigid silence of "cold conflict" mentioned in Chapter 15, in which even everyday courtesy and communication ("Would you pass me the salt?") has disappeared. It is quite the opposite: the former inhibits the growth of conflict (and leaves the door open for its reduction) while the latter keeps it eternally frozen in time. A further note on the importance of common courtesy. As discussed in Chapter 15, I recommend never allowing the situation to deteriorate to a point where even this is lost. For example, no matter how much our feelings are hurt, to write at least "Dear ..." when addressing someone in a written message (never just the name); to always end a letter with an appropriate sign-off and react to "Could you pass the salt?" with "Certainly!". The more often we take the moral high ground, the more confident we will feel about ourselves. Write this down in your conflict notebook as a promise to yourself! "No matter how fierce the conflict, I will never become caught up to the point of abandoning basic human decency!"

18.4 Resisting the temptation to demonise

The temptation to demonise others is a personal challenge. There is a strong tendency to attribute the behaviour of the other person to some inherent psychopathological element of their nature – after all, aren't they "really" simply "stupid, sick or evil"?[80] Distrust lies beneath this demonising view. Something inherently negative is projected onto the other party, however they behave (it is not difficult to recognise the hostile attribution error from Section 9.2 here). Those who decide to stop demonising the other party and are, for instance, willing to take unilateral measures on their own initiative to reduce tension, expose themselves to a certain risk (see Section 11.4). "Trust is much easier to turn into mistrust than mistrust into trust" (Luhmann, 1989, p. 99). At these

---

80 I confess that I am not immune to such thoughts myself – beyond the theory, this is after all an "easy way out" but it remains dangerous because it fosters escalation.

points, the conflict system is very vulnerable; a negative reaction from the other person can quickly turn the mood to resignation: "You see, I tried in good faith, but it's just no use!"

As already mentioned, "trusting in another's good intentions"[81] always means "taking a risk" (Luhmann, 1989, p. 23). But to choose to go into a situation with trust does not mean to trust blindly or naively. We do not lose our ability to discern but just open ourselves up to the possibility of a different perspective. Our willingness to assume that the other party has good intentions can be shown by trying to understand their perspective. Combined with this, an "asymmetry of attack" (i.e. not responding to an escalation with a stronger counter-escalation) can help to further defuse the climate of mistrust.

18.5 Mind your language!

Sometimes it might be better to assume that those situations in which people understand each other are actually the exceptions to the rule. We may be better off thinking of misunderstandings as the rule and appreciating moments of understanding for the special gift that they are. This is somewhat exaggerated but cannot be dismissed out of hand, especially when it comes to the restrictive conditions of conflict. Here, the number and severity of misunderstandings are likely to increase significantly, not least because we often quickly, almost unconsciously, scan the other party's words for anything that might be construed as an attack on our self-esteem (sometimes it only takes the first few words to set us off). It's a short internal check – "Can I let this stand or should I correct it or even counterattack?" It is therefore often advisable, especially for conflicting parties, to engage in forms of non-violent communication that reduce the risk of the other person feeling personally attacked (Omer & von Schlippe, 2023; Rosenberg, 2015).

In essence, this is also about awareness, especially in conflict. People use language to interact in different ways:[82] some use it to mark personal boundaries, to make it clear where they stand and what is important to them (see Figure 26). The form in which this may be done constructively is usually the classic "I" message ("This is getting too much for me now! I need a break!"). In contrast, language

---

81 A sentence for the conflict notebook: I often received feedback in conversations that this sentence, once it had come up in the conversation, appeared again and again in the thoughts of those seeking advice: "Taking the risk of assuming the other person has good intentions ...".
82 Although language can of course be used for simple information exchange, I refer here to its use in interpersonal communication.

can invade the personal space of the other person via "You" messages which devalue them or attribute negative motives to them ("You're doing this just to get back at me because you're a bad person!") (see Section 9.1). The other person experiences this as an "invasion of their private sphere", as a deeply hurtful attack on who and what they are – and nobody likes to be on the receiving end of that.

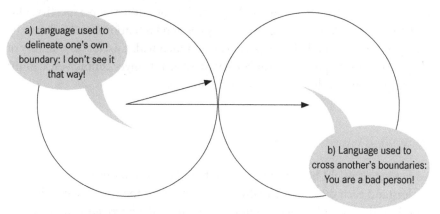

Figure 26: Different forms of the use of language in contact (source: own)

18.6 Symbolic gestures and good moments

The benefits of small gestures of goodwill have already been discussed in connection with the hostile perception error (Chapter 9). It may be difficult to take such a step in an escalated situation. Sometimes it helps to realise that it is usually the psychologically stronger party who makes such gestures. They must not appear to be appeasement. Offered independently of the other person's behaviour, they can be particularly powerful (Fisher et al., 2011; Omer & von Schlippe, 2023). They may simply be kind words, a handshake with a smile, an expression of regret (see Chapter 18) or even a small gift such as a magazine containing an article of interest. Such gestures can help defuse emotionally charged situations, express a willingness to improve the relationship, or simply demonstrate that we are not willing to be completely dominated by the conflict. However, as already emphasised, we should be prepared for the other person to reject the gesture; they may not automatically also be in a de-escalatory mode. The more we react calmly to rejection, the better the de-escalating effect. The importance of this awareness can be seen in the following story:

Symbolic gestures and good moments   165

A group of five adult siblings had fallen out hopelessly. The relationship between Rolf, one of the brothers, and Simone, his sister, was especially dire. Their father had been in touch with the institute where I work, and thus they had gained access to a series of texts on conflict issues (see https://www.wifu.de/en/wifu-library/). As I heard later, at the suggestion of Heike, another sister, they had begun to work through these together in several workshops. They read sections together and discussed to what extent the mechanisms depicted there applied to them. Heike later reported on a scene in which Simone had offered to look after her brother's child so that he could go to the cinema with his wife. Rolf had rejected this as a "cheap trick", which had offended Simone deeply. When they came across the topic of the "hostile perception error" while reading together, Rolf suddenly realised that he had fallen for this mechanism: "Hey, that's exactly what happened between us!" He apologised to Simone and that was the starting point for an improvement in relations.

It's not necessary to go to quite those lengths to improve relationships. Social relationships in which people feel comfortable with each other contain small, repeated "good moments". The Dutch therapist Maria Aarts has worked a great deal with parents and their children and has supported them to fill their days with moments in which both sides can feel good together: "A good moment makes a better day, a better day makes a better week, a better week helps to create a better life" (Maria Aarts in Hawellek, 2014, p. 43; see also https://www.martemeo.com/en/). Opportunities for these moments present themselves even when we are in conflict with the other person – although of course not as frequently or easily.

Figure 27: Friendly gestures – and good moments ... (Drawing and copyright: Björn von Schlippe)

A variant of the "friendly gestures approach ... can also be to make it clear to the other person again and again that we do want to improve the relationship (only if this is really the case, of course). A statement such as: "However we stand with each other at the moment, I am interested in having a better relationship with you!" makes the gesture, without admitting defeat or furthering an escalation. Here, too, we should be prepared for the answer to be "But I'm not!" and then remain friendly and relaxed and not let the other person's reaction tempt us to change our tone: "I don't know if you believe me, but I really mean it!"; "Anyway, I just wanted to let you know!" De-escalation can require persistence.[83] Accordingly, these small gestures need to be given again and again.

It takes time for the hostile perception error to fade. Any means by which we signal that we are interested in improving the relationship can potentially help to break the vicious circle of escalation. As with everything else, however, there is no guarantee that it will work, but with sensitivity, effort and time, there is a greater likelihood of at least small improvements.

18.7 Regrets

One gesture that can take on a special meaning is, as briefly indicated in Chapter 15, expressing regret about own actions or statements. Like the use of the word "partly", we do not cede our position by expressing that we are sorry for individual actions or letting ourselves get carried away in the course of the escalation. It is important in this context to be linguistically precise and to distinguish an expression of regret from a request for forgiveness. The intention will be similar – a desire for a step towards reconciliation – but a request for forgiveness can be perceived by the other person as an imposition ("First she was so offensive, and now I'm supposed to forgive her for it!"). Thus, requests for forgiveness may be rejected or devalued. An explicit request for forgiveness should be reserved for moments when we take full responsibility for a mistake we have made that resulted in emotional or physical harm to someone else (Ury, 2000, p. 165 f.). In such a situation, a mere apology may not carry the necessary weight. At the same time, asking for forgiveness puts us completely in the other party's hands, as they then have the power to grant or reject it, but even if the request is rejected, we should not take it as an excuse to rekindle the conflict.

---

83 It should also be recognised that de-escalation demands a great deal from the person who is trying to achieve it. Therefore, it needs more than just permission for self-care but, rather, active encouragement to treat oneself kindly and also perhaps a network of supporters who do not reinforce the outrage but support the steps towards de-escalation.

Rather, we recognise how deeply the violation has affected the other person. The rejection is then accepted or linked with the question "How can we put things right again?" This can lead to reconciliation in the sense of "restorative justice" (Johnstone & Van Ness, 2013) with a possibility that the bitterness will disappear but this should then be the result of a whole process and exceed the significance of any one single small gesture.

Thus, it is usually safer (in terms of de-escalation) to express regrets as "I'm sorry" rather than "Forgive me". This puts the other person under no pressure. Even if they say, "I don't believe you", the sentence "I'm sorry!" can then be qualified: "I'm sorry! I can't control whether you believe me, but I really am sorry!" (at this point, please don't start a discussion!).

The act of expressing regret will not automatically spark forgiveness. When this is expected or even demanded, there is a danger of starting the outrage carousel again – "What more do you want? I said I was sorry." Give the apology with "no strings attached" and leave it up to the other to decide if or when they bestow forgiveness. It may take time, even though it can be difficult to not be completely absolved by an apology. You have done what you could do. The rest is not under your control.

19 Positions and interests: "Why is this important to you?"

Whenever it comes to a professional view of conflict, there is none finer than the Harvard model (Fisher et al., 2011; Ponschab, 2015, 2018; Ury, 2000; Shapiro, 2017). This complex concept of fact-based negotiation, developed by Professors Roger Fisher, William Ury, and Bruce Patton, who worked at Harvard Law School at the same time, cannot and should not be presented in detail here – as noted at the beginning of Part Three. However, the core idea is helpful and deserves to be mentioned, because it concerns consciousness: the distinguishing between *positions* (often expressed loudly and early on in the dispute) and the *interests* behind them (sometimes not even quite clear to those that hold them) can help to pull a dispute back from the brink of escalation and to focus the participants back to the actual matter at hand rather than escalating by attacking each other's self-esteem.

The authors assume that the more care the parties take to ensure that the conflict does not permanently damage or even destroy the relationship between them, the more successful the negotiation of the conflictual issues will be. In many cases, even after a conflict is over, those involved continue to have to interact with each other, so it's beneficial for all involved if old disputes are not continually being dredged up.

One way to achieve this can be for the conflict partners to see each other not as opponents who are trying to optimize their position in relation to the other, but rather as fellow problem solvers who are striving for results that take everyone's interests into account. To this end, it can be helpful to remain open and to not commit to a specific outcome from the outset ("I will never back down from my demand!"). Instead, the clearer both sides are about the interests *behind* their respective positions, the greater the likelihood that they will learn what is really important to the other (behind the factual demands, interests are often more concerned with recognition, appreciation or gratitude) and work together to accommodate it. This in turn increases the likelihood that they will work together as problem solvers to find mutually agreeable solutions. The most important question that one can ask oneself and others involved in any dispute in order to understand the interests that are hidden behind expressed wishes, positions and demands is: "Why is this important to you?" A nice example was told to me by a student from our university:

He had become increasingly annoyed that his flatmate in the shared flat left her dirty breakfast dishes in the sink. She categorically rejected his request to put the dishes in the dishwasher straight away. It took some time for the two of them to understand each other's interests: He was bothered by the fact that when the sink was full of dishes, he could no longer fill the kettle from the tap to make tea. To her, it was important not to have to face housework immediately after getting up and having breakfast – and dishwasher meant housework for her. The clarification led to them buying a separate bowl, which was placed next to the sink. She put the dishes there and he had enough space for the kettle.

It is an interesting paradox: the more we insist on the factual side of the positions, the more fiercely we fight; and inversely, the more clearly both sides talk about the interests that lie underneath the positions (often connected with their feelings), the more relaxed they become in addressing the factual side of things. Especially when the interests in question involve *basic needs* (such as self-esteem – see Chapter 8), we are particularly vulnerable. However, it is not considered a good idea to make concessions too quickly on our positions before the interests have become clear – the desire to appease the other party rarely leads anywhere (Fisher et al., 2019, p. 239). The example of the Camp David process already mentioned in Chapter 17 shows strikingly how agreement at the level of interests and the associated basic needs made it possible to find solutions that would not have been found if they had remained at the level of positions:

Israel had occupied the Sinai in the 1967 Six-Day War and had decided to retain control over the peninsula: this was a clear position and not negotiable (at first). The Egyptians, for their part, insisted just as strongly on the position that the Sinai was part of their national territory and that there would be no peace until this situation was restored. When the question of interests came to the table it showed that Israel was primarily concerned with security: An enemy army could reach the heart of Israel within a few hours if the Israelis were no longer in control of the area. Egypt, however, was concerned with the integrity of its own territory and with exercising sovereign rights in its own country. Among many other issues (e. g., the settlements), the core of the plan that the leaders eventually agreed to was that Israel would return the Sinai, but that it would be demilitarised to a large extent: "The Egyptian flag was to fly over the entire peninsula, but Egyptian tanks were to stay away from the Israeli border" (Fisher et al., 2019, p. 77; see also Wright, 2016).

20 The balcony perspective and the blind spot

> *"Everything we see could also be otherwise. Everything we can describe at all could also be otherwise"* (Wittgenstein, 1968, Tractatus 5.634).
> *"To observe yourself means change yourself!"* (Alain, 1994).

20.1 Self-observation

Viewing an event – and oneself – from the "balcony perspective" (a term from the Harvard model) opens up the possibility that "things can be different" (Watzlawick, 1977). Events take on a different meaning when we change perspective. Conflict parties observe each other very closely and they also observe themselves – this is also referred to as "concurrent self-reference": A (psychological or social) system observes itself and how it relates to the environment.

Every observation inevitably brings certain parts into focus, while at the same time blurring other aspects: in this way often the highlighting of one aspect of a situation comes at the expense of the awareness of other aspects. "When we are in the process of observing, we cannot at the same time observe how we observe" (von Schlippe & Schweitzer, 2019, p. 110). Thus, every observation has its own blind spots (see Chapter 10). Adopting a balcony perspective is an explicit attempt to look at events through another lens – thereby creating the possibility of becoming aware of one's own blind spots by looking back at one's own process of observation – one's own thinking – from an "outside" perspective. Thus, in the spirit of the initial Wittgenstein quote, one can ask oneself how the world might be seen differently from one's habitually entrenched view. In this book, we have already discussed on various occasions how engrained the mutual perceptions can be and how fiercely the opponents sometimes fight against the possibility of seeing things differently ("You don't know her, she is like that!"). And yet it can be so interesting to adopt another point of view: so why not try out the following example for yourself?

Sit on a chair facing another (empty) chair opposite to you. Imagine that on that chair you are sitting as the person you will be when you retire (or when you are ninety years old, or whatever). You can also imagine a completely different person sitting on that chair, perhaps your father or mother, a wise hermit, or even your conflict partner. Now change seats and "become" that person. What does he/she tell you about the current conflict, and the escalation? How does she describe your own behaviour and that of the other conflict party; what recommendations do they give you? (i.e.: what recommendations do you give yourself from this other perspective)?

This little exercise might be helpful even if no other person is present as a supporter (it is similar to the suggestion presented in Section 18.1 to "step out of yourself" and in order to find new ways to move forward).

20.2 The carousel of expectations

The "carousel of expectations"[84] (not to be confused with the "carousel of indignation") enables us to manage more complex contexts in a similar way and to search for new perspectives and illuminate blind spots on one's own or with the support of a colleague or a coach.

The basic form is simple: With a particular problematic issue in mind, you take some time and sit down in the middle of a circle of chairs. Then, think about which people are significant in a particular topic – in any conflict, these are usually not only the main opponents, but often other third parties as well. And finally, consider which "inner figures" – your own "inner parts or voices" – could play a role here. For each of the external and internal figures, put a piece of paper with the corresponding name around yourself (= the "carousel"), then select the two, three or four most problematic figures and identify with them (you may do this by taking their "seat"). Then try to formulate what you believe to be the most important expectation of the person (or the internal figure) in question. Afterwards, sit down again on your own seat in the middle and search for a concise answer to that expectation (for details see von Schlippe, 2022c,

---

84 As you can see, I like using the carousel metaphor to illustrate circular processes! This particular carousel is a little exercise developed in the context of supervision of family therapeutic work, and later in coaching managers and company successors (von Schlippe, 2022c). In these professional contexts, people quickly find themselves exposed to a plethora of different expectations and interests. Originally, I had called the concept the "task carousel". But "carousel of expectations" fits better, since it does not involve only professional contexts and explicit commissions.

p. 332 ff.; von Schlippe & Jansen, 2020). The possibilities to "pull yourself out of the quagmire by your own bootstraps" in this way are of course limited, but in any case, you can gain some clarity about the many expectations to which you are exposed.

I remember a situation in which someone told me about a very derogatory comment that a third party had made about me. Since this third party was someone with whom I was professionally involved at various levels, I was deeply affected by it and took this feeling "home with me". Since it didn't go away on its own, I tried the expectation carousel. Quickly there were several pieces of paper (in this case I didn't use chairs) around me, some of them bearing the names of people from my past, also several stern inner voices (mostly you find 2-4 of these). That alone helped me understand why this remark had struck me so powerfully. The most striking experience for me, however, was to sit down in the place of the person in question and to take my time to identify with him and to feel how he might have experienced himself in relation to me (note that I had no direct contact with him at this point, the remark had been reported to me). Quite unlike what I had expected, I did not feel a cold arrogance on his chair (as I had assumed), but something that had not been accessible to me at all from the perspective of my own place: I experienced a strong feeling of fear in the other person's chair, it took some time until I was able to process my surprise. Apparently, I had found a way to understand a little more about the competitive relationship between us. Whether the person really was afraid, I never knew. But my own sense of being threatened had disappeared and I felt able to act towards the person again.

20.3 The reflecting team

One way of using the principle of "observing one's own observations" and illuminating possible blind spots professionally is a culture of systemic practice that has become known as the "reflecting team" through the work of Tom Andersen (Andersen, 1987, see also von Schlippe & Schweitzer, 2015). It has already been mentioned several times in this book (e.g. in Section 6.2 and in Chapter 12 we mentioned it as an instrument to slow down "high-speed communication"). Its form is simple (though not necessarily easy to implement): The conversation space is divided into two areas. One is the counselling space, where a counsellor and those seeking advice sit. In another part of the room, openly visible, sits a team (usually two to three people, co-therapists) that follows the conversation (remember the metaphor of the balcony, from which the conversation might be observed from a different perspective). The interview starts in the counselling group and is interrupted once or twice for a reflecting talk. The observers now talk to each other about their thoughts, ideas, associations, and feelings that emerged while listening to that talk. The interviewer (therapist) and the people seeking advice listen. It is important to note that the observers do not directly address the counselling group, because this setting should give the group members the opportunity to reflect on themselves without any pressure by just listening to the team's reflection. The setting is a kind of surprise to the people, as we are not used to such a constellation. Figure 28 brings this into a picture: In relaxed listening, we see ourselves in the "mirror" of the team's thoughts and reflections, so to speak, without having to immediately comment on or correct what has been said. It is like walking past an open door and hearing your own name: it is much more exciting to stop and listen than to go in and say: "Here I am ...". The reflections expressed in the observation room are taken up and are dropped more easily than if the people concerned were addressed directly (described in detail in Andersen, 1987; Caby, 2014; Hargens & von Schlippe, 1998).

Figure 28: Balcony perspective: The people concerned think about themselves while listening to others reflecting on them (drawing and copyright: Björn von Schlippe)

20.4 Reflective positions

Taking the principle of observation and perspective changing seriously, the key to this approach is not that there are experts sitting in the room contributing their professional thoughts. The real power lies in the changing of perspective, not in the "smart" people and what they say. Therefore, in a similar way, we can also invite those seeking advice to adopt the position of an observer toward themselves; we then speak of "reflective positions" (Drews et al., 2021).

The conversation is usually interrupted once or twice – by changing the setting together with the participants (who, of course, are introduced into the method and have agreed to it before). The participants sit down on different chairs and adopt the balcony perspective to look at the conversation and begin a "meta-talk" from a "higher level". The counsellor ensures that those involved remain in the meta-perspective, i.e., that they talk about the talk and don't simply continue the argument. This can be underscored by a small challenge: "I'm not sure if this might be too challenging, but I see a possibility in changing the setting. We could go to that sofa over there and imagine that we have been observers of the talk so far. We then could have a 'conversation about our conversation' from there. But that would mean that we all talk about ourselves sitting there as observers. Do you think we will be able to manage that?" Usually, the clients agree.

It is of course important that the professional facilitator is alert to anyone falling out of observation mode and back into conflict mode ("Well, that's a pretty stupid idea, idiot!")", and then, in a friendly but pointed way, asks whether it wouldn't be better to return to the other seats: "I'm sorry, maybe that was indeed too challenging for you after all …!" Usually, one such hint is enough to persuade the participants to follow the rules of meta-talk.

When in the "observation room" (= the sofa or other chairs), different rules apply. The focus is now the conversation itself, giving rise to a new and different set of questions:
- What could we use this new kind of observing our conversation from another perspective for now?
- If you had to choose a headline for that talk over there, what would it be?
- Imagine you have observed the conversation over there from here. How does it feel to be in this position? Are you annoyed, excited, pleased or shaken?
- Do you have the impression that the folks over there are making progress in the way they deal with each other?
- What associations come to mind when you think about the course of the conversation? Where are you curious to hear more, where do you stumble? Do you think they're on a good path or do we need the UN to intervene?

- Correspondingly, the consultant may also bring in own observations: "I was confused at that point ... Did you feel the same way?"

Example:
The first conversation with the two brothers from the family business mentioned in Chapter 9 had been highly charged from the start (for details, see von Schlippe & Quistorp, 2020), so my colleague and I suggested that we first talk to each brother individually. When the four of us then returned to the consulting room, we suggested that we first talk together in a different place from the "neutral observer position" over there – we would look at the table around where we had been sitting during the conversation. Would both be willing to do this? A clear "yes" comes as an answer.

The reflection between the brothers and the consultants now took place on an equal footing jointly as four observers. The quality of the conversation changes significantly, the tension decreases, and interesting comments are made about the course of the conversation, the critical points and pitfalls. For example, Michael (the younger brother), when asked: "As a consultant, what would you advise that Michael over there, whom you know particularly well, should do? What could his contribution be to give the talk a positive twist?", answered: "Well, I would advise him to maybe stop always wanting to change his brother – and accept him more as he is, with all his weaknesses!" Manfred (the elder brother), when asked what advice he would give, if he were his own advisor, suggested making his brother the chairman of the advisory board. By observing themselves in the reflective position, they gained access to a much wider range of possibilities. Back at the table the negotiation of the conflict issues was much more constructive.

The procedures presented in the second part of this chapter clearly have a methodical side, but from my point of view, the possibility of the quality of consciousness that arises from a relaxed playing with perspectives is essential. It surprises me again and again how even in violent and tense situations the atmosphere is changed by adopting the balcony perspective. I usually now introduce the possibility of the "balcony" already in the initial consultation; the green sofa in my study is then the place where I suggest going for such a reflection conversation. If I have a consultation appointment elsewhere, I always ask to put at least three more chairs than participants in the room, so that we can easily turn a corner into an "observation room".

21 The "third element"

21.1 A person or principle as "the third party"

> *"The lion will lie down with the lamb if only it rains hard enough"* (Bateson, 1972, p. 81).

Conflicts rarely take place between two people/parties alone, usually, third parties are involved in some form. These can exacerbate the conflict; for example, an escalation may be in the interests of a lawyer; a grandfather or a mother-in-law interfere in a marriage by making irritating remarks; friends may give advice that intensifies the escalation, and so on. It can therefore be helpful to think about possible influences of such third parties in the conflict and to ask about their impact (and perhaps even invite them to join the talk).

Even more interesting, however, is that a "third element" – and this does not necessarily have to be a person or a group – can also ensure the *limitation of* a symmetrical escalation (see Chapter 1), i.e., it can prevent or interrupt an ever-increasing dispute.

The American mediator William Ury describes a small scene in which an argument escalated quickly when a car driver, who was driving very fast towards a group of people and only braked at the last moment, reacted with the utmost indignation to the fact that one of the group had struck his fist on the car bonnet in fright and anger. A loud argument developed; others joined in … The driver was a black man, the others white, so the dispute quickly took on a racist edge. Suddenly, the disputants noticed an older man behind them who kept slowly moving his hands up and down in a calming gesture, "Okay, now, cool it!" The driver went back to his car and drove off without another word, and the crowd dispersed. Ury says: "He was an archetypical 'third side'", that is, in its basic form, a third party acting positively (Ury, 2000, p. 4).

Gregory Bateson had written about this "third element" decades ago (Bateson, 1972, p. 80 ff.). A limiting factor can stop an escalating spiral in its tracks – though probably it would take a "very heavy rain" to ensure that "lion and lamb lie peacefully together". But the fact that an external threat can represent a third factor that can stop some disputes or turn them around will be familiar to anyone who has ever wanted to stop an argument between two people and experienced how quickly they can ally against him: "Don't you get involved!"

Sometimes even the simple physical presence of a witness who is just "there" is enough. For example, in systemic parent coaching, parents who are ashamed of their adolescent child's violent behaviour are advised to give up secrecy and to "find at least one person outside of the family [...] who can act as a witness and tell the aggressor and the victim that they are aware of the facts and will support the parents to end the violence" (Omer & von Schlippe, 2023). It is hard to act in a massively invalidating or violent way when an outsider is present, even if they are just watching or listening. In the case of the aforementioned two brothers (see the example in Section 20.4), the mother had been such a third element for a long time:

Their father had died early and unexpectedly when the brothers were 26 and 24 years old. On his deathbed, he had said to his wife, "Take care that the boys don't fight, Mum!" By mutual agreement, one brother (they each had 50 % of the shares) had taken over the management of the company; the other brother was a silent partner. The mother had been a rather quiet person, she had been a member of the advisory board, but there she had rarely said anything at all. Somehow, the brothers later said, the mother's mere presence had a calming influence, in her quiet silence. However, the first fierce and irreconcilable dispute between the brothers already arose at her funeral – about a trivial matter, as both say. About six months later, a massive conflict erupted over the non-operational brother's ability to influence the company (abridged from von Schlippe, 2014c, p. 74 ff.). This example is reminiscent of the scene in Thomas Mann's *Buddenbrooks,* where the dispute between Thomas and his brother Christian also escalates at the mother's deathbed. The desperate sister, who points out that the dead mother is lying in the next room, does not manage to take over the role of the symmetry limiter, that the mother had held during her lifetime.

The third element, as already mentioned, does not necessarily have to be a living person. As Bateson says, it is simply something that curbs escalation between people or groups by uniting both sides into either loyalty or opposition to this third party (Bateson, 1981, p. 112). Possible aspects:
- Living people in the position of such a third party were already mentioned in the previous examples. Even deceased persons can fulfil such a func-

tion. Respect or affection may then become the "third" (a higher principle) that might limit the symmetry: "Come on, let's end this! Dad wouldn't have wanted this!"
- Looking back on a common history or shared values to which you refer, or looking forward to what you want to achieve together.
- It can also be something quite abstract that is experienced as greater than the opponents themselves. For example, both sides can recognise chance as a higher principle and an escalation is prevented if a coin is tossed in each case of dispute. Religious people consciously subordinate themselves to God as a greater power; couple conflicts can be mitigated by the fact that one of them backs off for the sake of their shared love, and so on.
- On a more abstract level, the introduction of institutions, from the legal system to the UN, is certainly worth mentioning here, too.

These examples (and more may be found in conflict talks) are attempts to create structures that moderate the destructive effect of unchecked escalating conflicts by developing a "third party" to which the parties ultimately (have to) bow – anyone who tries to continue the dispute afterwards has lost all legitimacy for it.[85]

If this symmetry-limiting third element disappears, perhaps even suddenly, the escalation may be sudden and violent. In his study, Grossmann found such system-irritating ruptures to be quite typical for escalating conflicts in family businesses: At the moment of such a rupture – such as the death of a close relative – a conflict dynamic that may have been latent for years can suddenly break out and then it becomes apparent how quickly the behaviour of those involved can escalate analogously to an arms race when the inhibiting factors cease to exist. "In this sense, the loss of such a limiting factor can unleash the forces of conflict and lead to the collapse of the system" (Grossmann & von Schlippe, 2015, p. 304).

---

[85] Especially after the Second World War, intensive work was done on a security architecture that was based on these principles and built strong institutions like the UN, the EU, the World Court of Justice in Den Haag, etc. These institutions fulfill since long the function of a "third element" that all other parties accept, but they are in danger. The recklessness with which these institutions are currently being questioned or even ignored from various sides is a worrying sign, because "programs and institutions are the backbones of the third side" (Ury, 2000, p. 212).

21.2 The importance of a grand gesture

One aspect that should at least be briefly touched on here is the possibility that a person who is broadly acknowledged with reputation and authority (e.g. a wise person or an elected leader) can take a decisive step to improve the situation by introducing a "grand gesture" as "third element". Interestingly, the person who makes this gesture does not even have to be external – it could also be one of the opponents who has enough credibility for such an action. This is often seen in gestures that have historical significance (though of course it is also conceivable that they could be significant in smaller contexts). An example:

In 1962, 17 years after the end of the Second World War, French President de Gaulle of France visited Germany. In a striking speech to the German young people, he said here, among other things, in German(!):

I extend my congratulations to you all! Firstly, I congratulate you for being young. One only has to see the fire in your eyes, to listen to the force of your convictions, witness the personal passion of every one of you and experience the common revival of your group to be convinced that this enthusiasm has chosen you to master your life and the future.

I congratulate you furthermore on being young Germans, by which is meant: the children of a great people. Yes indeed, of a great people that, in the course of its existence, has made great mistakes. A people that has also given to the world fruitful spiritual, scientific, artistic and philosophical works, and enriched it with countless products of its inventiveness, its technology and its work ethic.

A people that in its peaceful acts, as in the pain of war, has developed true riches of courage, discipline and organisation. The French people know to value this highly, as it also knows what it is to be happy to work and to create, to give and to suffer.

The speech was an important step in the reconciliation efforts of the two states, which had lived a bitter "hereditary enmity" for centuries.[86]

We can imagine the effect of such a grand gesture. Higher principles such as forgiveness, appreciation and understanding lent this particular speech such power. It may not be possible in an acute conflict, perhaps time must pass before such a gesture can unfold its full effectiveness. But in conflicts that are decades old, a courageous step could create that "third element" that might lead to a turning point. Mahatma Gandhi's famous Salt March, for example, was such a step; and the higher principle that gave himself and his followers legitimacy was the principle of nonviolence (Sharp, 1960). In the end, this was stronger

---

86 https://www.youtube.com/watch?v=t4kraOzcteM Link last accessed on Dec. 27th, 2023.

than military power – however, he had also judged the timing correctly; in a "hot" war, this gesture would certainly not have been successful. The Egyptian leader Anwar al Sadat also was a "master of the grand gesture" (Wright, 2016, p. 41) – his offer to come to Israel and address the Israeli parliament initiated the Camp David process (see Chapter 17). Again, it was not the act of a single person toward the enemy state, but rather the willingness of one of the conflict-parties to relate to and act upon something else – in this case the vision of genuine peace – that brought about the change.

There are many conceivable conflict hotspots in the world that could be significantly defused with such gestures (and as Camp David, for example, makes clear, if such gestures are made, they mark only the beginning, not the end, of a long and difficult process). Sadat was convinced that 70 % of the conflict between Israel and the Arabs was psychological in nature (Wright, 2016, p. 36). It is likely to be similar in other conflicts. But rarely do leaders have the vision to take the bold step to create a third element, a higher principle to which they also subordinate themselves.

PART FOUR: TEN RECOMMENDATIONS FOR DEALING WITH CONFLICTS

"So, it may well be that, in a certain sense, we are 'creatures of history', but in another sense we are autonomous actors" (Bruner, 1997, p. 118).

I would like to conclude this book with a list of ten recommendations, after which I hand the conflict notebook over to you, the reader, to continue it yourself. I created the list a few years ago at the University of Witten/Herdecke together with my friend and colleague Torsten Groth,[87] inspired by the work of Fritz Simon, Fritz Glasl, Haim Omer, Wolfgang Loth and many others. Here it is:

1. Remember: Every conflict requires at least two mutually hostile parties! You can only have an enemy if you have a clear image of them as enemies. Thus, the other person, the other party, is always, in part, a reflection of your view of them.
2. Keep in mind that once a conflict has arisen, it can become a "parasite" that increasingly determines communication dynamics and forms of perception. Be wary of its lures and aware of how you can resist them. In case of doubt, at first, do nothing, count up to one hundred (or one thousand) – or do "something else" – anything but allowing your emotions take over in the heat of the moment.
3. Mind your language. Talk in a de-escalating way, i.e. without invading the "inner space" of the other party, and of course without necessarily giving up your positions (e.g. formulate I-messages, needs, and wishes instead of accusing or making ultimate demands).

---

87 He has kindly allowed me to use this jointly updated list here.

4. Look for opportunities to express gestures of appreciation or your willingness to improve the relationship and reconcile (without necessarily giving in!). Anticipate that your counterpart will likely initially respond even to positive offers through the lens of the hostile perception error. React in a calm and relaxed manner: they don't need to accept; it doesn't take anything from your gesture if they don't ('I give you a rose and if you don't take it, it's still a rose!')!
5. It may sometimes be good to let the other person win in order to win yourself (e.g., when it comes to preserving the relationship: the relationship is the larger third element that you jointly relate to). So, check to see if there is not a third element that is of greater long-term relevance than the short-term struggle.
6. Check if it is a conflict that you can win at all. It is anyway questionable in many close relationships whether it is meaningful to engage in power struggles, but if you do, then you should at least be very sure you *can* win (and that the winning is worth what you risk losing)! In cases of doubt, you should rather overestimate the strength of your opponent! If the further course of the escalation is not predictable, get out! This is especially true if you realise that you are already willing to destroy the other person or even yourself to "win".
7. Assess the severity of the conflict. Is there a chance that the conflict system will find a solution on its own? Does it perhaps need a third party as a mediator? Or might the intervention of the "UN" even be necessary to stop the escalation in free fall?
8. Any mediator should be considered neutral (with respect to the conflict topic) not only by you but also by the other party. If you yourself are this third party, check whether both parties assign to you the role of a higher power (judge, decision maker, process shaper). Ensure an end to destructive processes and create a framework in which constructive events are possible. Maintain your neutrality and give the conflict parties responsibility for the continuation of the process.
9. Introduce your ideas for possible solutions in the form of questions without being overly attached to any of them.
10. Realise that solutions to conflicts are usually not logical or consistent. Endure ambiguity! Do not hold out for the "perfect" solution.

Even though conflicts confront us with the wide range of sensibilities and psychological mechanisms that we as human beings have acquired in the course of our developmental history, we are not automatons condemned to behave unquestioningly as the logic of the conflict dictates. We are also capable of acting as conscious actors. To do so, however, we must engage with the events that surround us consciously and with self-reflection. I hope that reading this book will help to deal with conflicts in a more sensitive and constructive way. Ultimately, you, as one of those concerned are also doing *yourself* some good: the energy consumed by outrage and indignation in riding the carousel can perhaps be put to better use elsewhere.

References

Alain (1994). *Sich beobachten heißt sich verändern*. Insel.
Ameln, F. von (2004). *Konstruktivismus: Die Grundlagen systemischer Therapie, Beratung und Bildungsarbeit*. Francke.
Anders, G. (1988). *Der Blick vom Turm. Fabeln* (3rd ed.). Beck.
Andersen, T. (1987), The Reflecting Team: Dialogue and meta-dialogue in clinical work. *Family Process*, 26: 415–428. https://doi.org/10.1111/j.1545-5300.1987.00415.x
Anter, A. (2012). *Theorien der Macht. Zur Einführung*. Junius.
Ashby, W. R. (1991). Requisite variety and its implications for the control of complex systems. In G. J. Klir (Ed.), *Facets of systems science* (pp. 405–417). Springer Science and Business Media.
Assmann, J. (1988). Kollektives Gedächtnis und kulturelle Identität. In J. Assmann & T. Hölscher (Eds.), *Kultur und Gedächtnis* (pp. 9–19). Suhrkamp.
Baecker, D. (1999). *Organisation als System*. Suhrkamp.
Ballreich, R. & Glasl, F. (2011). *Konfliktmanagement und Mediation in Organisationen*. Concadora.
Bateman, A. & Fonagy, P. (2015). *Handbuch Mentalisieren*. Psychosozial.
Bateson, G. (1972). *Steps to an ecology of mind*. University of Chicago Press.
Bateson, G. (1984). *Geist und Natur. Eine notwendige Einheit*. (3rd ed.). Suhrkamp. English version: 1979, *Mind and nature. A necessary unity*. Dutton.
Bateson, G. & Bateson, M. C. (1994). Wo Engel zögern. Unterwegs zu einer Epistemologie des Heiligen. English version: 1987, *Angels fear: Towards an epistemology of the sacred*. Macmillan Publishing Company
Bauer, J. & Marshall, E. (2009). The brain transforms psychology into biology. *Body, Movement and Dance in Psychotherapy*, 4:3, 231–238. DOI: 10.1080/17432970903322341
Baumeister, R. F. & Leary, M. R. (1995). The need to belong: Desire for interpersonal attachments as a fundamental human motivation. *Psychological Bulletin*, 117 (3), pp. 497–529.
Berry, Z. & Frederickson, J. (2015). Explanations and implications of the fundamental attribution error: A review and proposal. *Journal of Integrated Social Sciences*, 5(1), 44–57.
Bierhoff, H. W. (1992). Prozedurale Gerechtigkeit: Das Wie und Warum der Fairness. *Zeitschrift für Sozialpsychologie*, 23, 163–178.
Bonacker, T. (2008). Die Konflikttheorie der autopoietischen Systemtheorie. In *Sozialwissenschaftliche Konflikttheorien. Eine Einführung* (4th ed., pp. 267–291). VS Verlag für Sozialwissenschaften.
Bonacker, T. & Imbusch, P. (2004). Sozialwissenschaftliche Konfliktforschung. In G. Sommer & A. Fuchs (Eds.), *Krieg und Frieden. Handbuch der Konflikt- und Friedenspsychologie* (pp. 195–207). Beltz PVU.
Boothe, B. (2009). Die Geburt der Psyche im elterlichen Erzählen. *Familiendynamik*, 34(1), 30–43.
Boszormenyi-Nagy, I. & Spark, G. (1981). *Unsichtbare Bindungen. Die Dynamik familiärer Systeme*. Klett-Cotta. English version: 1973, *Invisible loyalties: Reciprocity in intergenerational family therapy*. Harper & Row.

References

Bregman, R. (2020). *Im Grunde gut: eine neue Geschichte der Menschheit.* Rowohlt.
Brosnan, S. F. & de Waal, F. B. M. (2003). Monkeys reject unequal pay. *Nature, 425*(6955), 297–299. https://doi.org/10.1038/nature01963
Bruner, J. (1997). *Sinn, Kultur und Ich-Identität.* Carl Auer Systeme. English version: 1990, *Acts of meaning.* Harvard University Press.
Bruner, J. (1998). Vergangenheit und Gegenwart als narrative Konstruktionen. In J. Straub (Ed.), *Erzählung, Identität und historisches Bewusstsein* (pp. 46–80). Suhrkamp.
Bruner, J. (1999). Self-making and world-making. Wie das Selbst und seine Welt autobiographisch hergestellt werden. *Journal für Psychologie, 1*(1), 11–12.
Burton, J. (1993) (Ed.). *Conflict: Human Needs Theory.* Palgrave MacMillan.
Caby, F. (2014). Reflektierendes Team. In T. Levold & M. Wirsching (Eds.), *Systemische Therapie und Beratung – das große Lehrbuch* (pp. 250–255). Carl Auer Systeme.
Catherall, D. R. (2022). Emotionale Sicherheit. Affektive Kommunikation in Paarbeziehungen und Paartherapie. English version: 2007. *Emotional safety: Viewing couples through the lens of affect.* Routledge.
Ciompi, L. (1997). The concept of affect logic: An integrative psycho-socio-biological approach. *Psychiatry, 60,* 158–170
Ciompi, L. (2004). Ein blinder Fleck bei Niklas Luhmann? Soziale Wirkungen von Emotionen aus Sicht der fraktalen Affektlogik. *Soziale Systeme, 10*(1), 21–49. https://doi.org/doi:10.1515/sosys-2004-0103
Ciompi, L. (2005). *Die emotionalen Grundlagen des Denkens. Entwurf einer fraktalen Affektlogik.* Vandenhoeck & Ruprecht.
Ciompi, L. (2021). *Ciompi reflektiert. Wissenschaftliches, Persönliches und Weltanschauliches aus der Altersperspektive.* Vandenhoeck & Ruprecht.
Ciompi, L. & Endert, E. (2011). *Gefühle machen Geschichte. Die Wirkung kollektiver Emotionen – von Hitler bis Obama.* Vandenhoeck & Ruprecht.
Ciompi, L. & Tschacher, W. (2021). Affect-Logic, embodiment, synergetics, and the free energy principle: New approaches to the understanding and treatment of schizophrenia. *Entropy* 23(12), 1619; https://doi.org/10.3390/e23121619
Clark, C. (2014). *The sleepwalkers: How Europe went to war in 1914.* Harper Perennial.
Colin, N. & Demesmay, C. (Eds.) (2021). *Franco-German relations seen from abroad. Frontiers in international relations.* Springer
Daft, R. L. & Lengel, R. H. (1983). *Information richness. A new approach to managerial behavior and organization design.* Texas A and M Univ College Station Coll of Business Administration.
Daft, R. L. & Lengel, R. H. (1986). Organizational information requirements, media richness and structural design. *Management Science, 32*(5), 554–571.
Das, D. & Neog, R. (2020). Language game: Ludwig Wittgenstein. *International Journal of Management* 11(12), 143–148. Article ID: IJM_11_12_016
Davis, J. A., Hampton, M. M., & Lansberg, I. (1997). *Generation to generation: Life cycles of the family business.* Harvard Business Press.
Dobbs, M. (2008). *One Minute to Midnight: Kennedy, Khrushchev and Castro on the brink of nuclear war.* Random House.
Dodge, K. A. (2006). Translational science in action: Hostile attributional style and the development of aggressive behavior problems. *Development and Psychopathology, 18*(03), 791–814. https://doi.org/10.1017/S0954579406060391
Drews, A., Born, M., & Schlippe, A. von (2021). Reflektierende Positionen im Therapieprozess. In B. Strauß, M. Galliker, M. Linden, & J. Schweitzer (Eds.), *Ideengeschichte der Psychotherapie. Theorien, Konzepte, Methoden* (pp. 328–334). Kohlhammer.
Eidelson, R. J. & Eidelson, J. I. (2003). Dangerous ideas: Five beliefs that propel groups toward conflict. *American Psychologist, 58,* 182–192.

Eidenschink, K. (2023). *Die Kunst des Konflikts. Konflikte schüren und beruhigen lernen*. Heidelberg: Carl Auer Systeme

Elovainio, M., Kivimäki, M., & Vahtera, J. (2002). Organizational justice: evidence of a new psychosocial predictor of health. *American Journal of Public Health, 92*(1), 105–108.

Festinger, L. (1954). A theory of social comparison processes. *Human Relations, 7,* 117–140.

Fischer, C. (2019). Der Ziegenfall – rechtstheoretische Betrachtungen zu "Gerechtigkeit in der Mediation." In C. Fischer (Ed.), *Kommunikation im Konflikt* (1st ed., pp. 129–145). Beck.

Fischer, H. R. (2012). Die Verflüssigung des Denkens. Vom Aufsetzen einer neuen Denkbrille. *Familiendynamik 37*(2), 148–152.

Fischer, H. R. (2021). *Sprache, Grammatik und Lebensform. Wittgensteins Beitrag zur Philosophie der Psychologie* (3rd revise). Wiss. Buchgesellschaft.

Fisher, R. (1989). *The social psychology of intergroup and international conflict resolution*. Springer.

Fisher, R. (1997). *Interactive conflict resolution*. Syracuse University Press.

Fisher, R., Ury, W. L., & Patton, B. (2011). *Getting to yes: Negotiating agreement without giving in*. Penguin. German version: (2019). *Das Harvard-Konzept* (2nd ed.). Deutsche Verlags Anstalt.

Förstl, H. (2012). *Theory of mind: Neurobiologie und Psychologie sozialen Verhaltens* (2nd ed.). Springer.

Fries, A. & Grawe, K. (2006). Inkonsistenz und psychische Gesundheit: Eine Metaanalyse. *Zeitschrift für Psychiatrie, Psychologie und Psychotherapie, 54*(2), 133–148. https://doi.org/10.1024/1661-4747.54.2.133

Frisch, M. (1964). Tagebuch 1946–1949. Suhrkamp.

Fuchs, P. (1993). *Moderne Kommunikation: zur Theorie des operativen Displacements*. Suhrkamp.

Gareis, S. B., Kulessa, M., Hasse, R., Glasl, F., & Brzoska, M. (2014). Sanktionen gegen Russland – ein kluges politisches Instrument? *S&F Sicherheit und Frieden, 32*(4), 265–273.

Gehmann, U. (2016). Myths and narratives for management. *International Business Research 9*(1), 123–135.

Glasl, F. (2002). *Confronting conflict. A first-aid kit for handling conflict*. Athenaeum Press.

Glasl, F. (2013). *Konfliktmanagement: Ein Handbuch zur Diagnose und Behandlung von Konflikten für Organisationen und ihre Berater* (11th ed.). Haupt.

Glasl, F. (2014a). Der heimliche Krieg. Wie können wir mit der Dynamik kalter Konflikte konstruktiv umgehen? *Konfliktdynamik, 3*(2), 101–109.

Glasl, F. (2014b). Eskalationsdynamik – zur Logik von Affektsteigerungen. *Konfliktdynamik, 3*(3), 190–199.

Gottman, J. M. (1993). A theory of marital dissolution and stability. *Journal of family psychology, 7*(1), 57–75. doi:10.1037/0893-3200.7.1.57.

Gottman, J. M. (1994). *What predicts divorce? The relationship between marital processes and marital outcomes*. Lawrence Erlbaum.

Gottman, J. M. (1995). *Why marriages succeed and fail*. Fireside.

Gottman, J. M. & Levenson, R. W. (2000). The timing of divorce: Predicting when a couple will divorce over a 14-year period. *Journal of Marriage and Family, 62*(3), 737–745.

Grabbe, M., Jürgens, G., & Schlippe, A. von (1998). »Als würden wir gemeinsam einen Teppich weben …«. Reflektierendes Team in einer systemtherapeutischen Lehrpraxis. In J. Hargens & A. von Schlippe (Eds.), *Das Spiel der Ideen. Reflektierendes Team und systemische Praxis* (151–177). Modernes Lernen.

Grimley, B. (2013). *Theory and practice of NLP coaching. A psychological approach*. London: Sage.

Grizelj, M. (2012). Medien. In O. Jahraus, A. Nassehi, M. Grizelj, & et al. (Eds.), *Luhmann Handbuch. Leben, Werk, Wirkung* (pp. 99–101). Metzler.

Grossmann, St. & Schlippe, A. von (2015) Conflict in family businesses – Family businesses: Fertile environments for conflict. *Journal of Family Business Management 5*(2), 294–314.

Groth, T. (2017). *66 Gebote systemischen Denkens und Handelns in Management und Beratung*. Carl Auer Systeme.

References

Gupta-Carlson, H. (2016). Re-Imagining the nation: Storytelling and social media in the Obama campaigns. *Political Science & Politics, 49*(1), 71–75.
Hahn, A. (1983). Konsensfiktionen in kleinen Gruppen. Dargestellt am Beispiel von jungen Ehen. In F. Neidhardt (Ed.), *Gruppensoziologie. Perspektiven und Materialien. Sonderheft 25 der Kölner Zeitschrift für Soziologie und Sozialpsychologie* (pp. 210–232). Westdeutscher Verlag.
Haita-Falah, C. (2017). Sunk-cost fallacy and cognitive ability in individual decision-making. *Journal of Economic Psychology, 58,* 44–59.
Haken, H. (1992). Synergetics in Psychology. In W. Tschacher et al. (Eds.) *Self-organization and clinical psychology. Empirical approaches to synergetics in psychology* (pp. 32–54). Springer.
Hamilton, O. S. & Lordan, G. (2023). Ability or luck: A systematic review of interpersonal attributions of success. *Frontiers in Psychology, 13,* 8220.
Hargens, J. & Schlippe, A. von (Eds.) (1998). *Das Spiel der Ideen. Reflektierendes Team und systemische Praxis* (2nd ed.). Borgmann.
Harvey, M. & Evans, R. E. (1994). Family business and multiple levels of conflict. *Family Business Review, 7*(4), 331–348. https://doi.org/10.1111/j.1741-6248.1994.00331.x
Hawellek, C. (2014). Einladung zum Perspektivwechsel. *Familiendynamik, 39*(1), 38–49.
Heisenberg, W. (1955). *Das Naturbild der heutigen Physik.* Rowohlt.
Hertel, A. von (2013). *Professionelle Konfliktlösung. Führen mit Mediationskompetenz* (2nd ed.). Campus.
Hochschild, A. R. (2016). The ecstatic edge of politics: Sociology and Donald Trump. *Contemporary Sociology, 45*(6), 683–689. https://doi.org/10.1177/0094306116671947
Hochschild, A. (2017). *Fremd in ihrem Land.* Campus. English version: 2018, *Strangers in their own land: Anger and mourning on the American right.* New Press.
Hülsbeck, M. & Schlippe, A. von (2018). Die Rolle psychologischer Kontrakte für die Entstehung von Konflikten. *Konfliktdynamik, 7*(2), 92–101.
Imber-Black, E. (1999). *The secret life of families: Making decisions about secrets.* Random House.
Jakob, P., Borcsa, M., Olthof, J., & Schlippe, A. von (Eds.) (2022). *Narrative Praxis. Ein Handbuch für Beratung, Therapie und Coaching.* Vandenhoeck & Ruprecht.
Janis, I. (1991). Groupthink. In *A first look at communication theory* (pp. 235–246). McGrawHill.
Janis, I. (2011). Groupthink: The desperate drive for consensus at any cost. In J. Shafritz, J. Ott, & J. Yong (Eds.), *Classics of organization theory* (pp. 189–196). Cengage Learning.
Jansen, T., & Vogd, W. (2013). Polykontexturale Verhältnisse – disjunkte Rationalitäten am Beispiel von Organisationen. *Zeitschrift für theoretische Soziologie, 2*(1), 82–97.
Jehn, K. A. (1997). A qualitative analysis of conflict types and dimensions in organizational groups. *Administrative Science Quarterly, 42*(3), 530–557.
Jehn, K. A. (2014). Types of conflict: The history and future of conflict definitions and typologies. In O. B. Ayoko, N. M. Ashkanasy, & K. A. Jehn (Eds.), *Handbook of conflict management research* (pp. 3–18). Edward Elgar Publishing.
Johnstone, G., & Van Ness, D. (Eds.) (2013). *Handbook of restorative justice.* Routledge.
Jonas, E., Schulz-Hardt, S., & Frey, D., Thelen, N. (2001). Confirmation bias in sequential information search after preliminary decisions: an expansion of dissonance theoretical research on selective exposure to information. *Journal of Personality and Social Psychology, 80*(4), 557–571
Kalisch, D. E. (2007). *Empörung. Psychologische Grundlagen ihrer gezielten Veränderung.* Dr. Kovac.
Kaye, K. (1996). When the family business is a sickness. *Family Business Review, 9*(4), 347–368. https://doi.org/10.1111/j.1741-6248.1996.00347.x
Kellermanns, F. W. & Eddleston, K. A. (2007). A family perspective on when conflict benefits family firm performance. *Journal of Business Research, 60*(10), 1048–1057.
Keltner, D. (2016). *Das Macht-Paradox: wie wir Einfluss gewinnen oder verlieren.* Campus.
Kidwell, R. E., Kellermanns, F. W., & Eddleston, K. A. (2012). Harmony, justice, confusion, and conflict in family firms: Implications for ethical climate and the "fredo effect". *Journal of business ethics, 106,* 503–517.

Kleve, H. (2017). Reziprozität ermöglichen. Vernetzung aus systemtheoretischer Perspektive. *Kontext, 48*(4), 353–367.

Kleve, H. (2020). *Die Unternehmerfamilie. Wie Wachstum, Sozialisation und Beratung gelingen.* Carl Auer Systeme.

Kochinka, A. (2015). *Emotionstheorien: Begriffliche Arbeit am Gefühl.* transcript. https://doi.org/doi:10.1515/9783839402351

Krastev, I., & Holmes, S. (2019). *Das Licht, das erlosch. Eine Abrechnung.* Ullstein.

Kriz, J. (2009). Cognitive and interactive patterning: Processes of creating meaning. In J. Valsiner, P. C. Molenaar, M. Lyra, & N. Chaudhary (Eds.), *Dynamic process methodology in the social and developmental sciences* (pp. 619–650). Springer.

Kriz, J. (2017a). Hermann Hakens Synergetik als Grundmodell für das Verständnis des Menschen in der Welt. In J. Kriz & W. Tschacher (Eds.), *Synergetik als Ordner* (pp. 85–94). Pabst.

Kriz, J. (2017b). *Subjekt und Lebenswelt. Personzentrierte Systemtheorie für Psychotherapie, Beratung und Coaching.* Vandenhoeck & Ruprecht.

Kriz, J., Lück, H., & Heidbrink, H. (1987). *Wissenschafts- und Erkenntnistheorie.* Leske & Budrich.

Laing, R., Philipson, H., & Lee, A. (1973). *Interpersonelle Wahrnehmung.* Suhrkamp. English version: 1966, *Interpersonal perception.* Tavistock Publications.

Lau, B. K. Y., Geipel, J., Wu, Y., & Keysar, B. (2022). The extreme illusion of understanding. *Journal of experimental psychology. General, 151*(11), 2957–2962.

LeDoux, J. (1998). *Das Netz der Gefühle.* Hanser. English version: 1998, *The emotional brain: The mysterious underpinnings of emotional life.* Simon and Schuster.

Lerner, M. J. (1977). The justice motive in social behavior. Some hypotheses as to its origins and forms. *Journal of Personality, 45*, 1–52.

Lerner, M. J. (1980). *The belief in a just world: A fundamental delusion.* Plenum Press.

Lindemann, G. (2006). Die Emergenzfunktion und die konstitutive Funktion des Dritten. *Zeitschrift für Soziologie, 35*(2), 82–101.

Lindemann, H., Mayer, C.-H., & Osterfeld, I. (2018). *Systemisch-lösungsorientierte Mediation und Konfliktklärung.* Vandenhoeck & Ruprecht.

Luhmann, N. (1981). Die Unwahrscheinlichkeit der Kommunikation. In N. Luhmann (Ed.), *Soziologische Aufklärung 3: Soziales System, Gesellschaft, Organisation* (pp. 25–34). VS Verlag für Sozialwissenschaften.

Luhmann, N. (1989). *Vertrauen. Ein Mechanismus der Reduktion sozialer Komplexität.* Lucius & Lucius.

Luhmann, N. (1995). *Social systems.* Stanford University Press.

Luhmann, N. (1996). Widerspruch und Konflikt. In T. Bonacker (Ed.), *Konflikttheorien. Eine sozialwissenschaftliche Einführung* (pp. 477–494). Leske & Budrich.

Luhmann, N. (2000). *Organisation und Entscheidung.* Westdeutscher Verlag.

Luhmann, N. (2005). Sozialsystem Familie. In N. Luhmann (Ed.), *Soziologische Aufklärung 5. Konstruktivistische Perspektiven* (3rd ed., pp. 189–209). VS Verlag für Sozialwissenschaften.

Luhmann, N. (2008). Die Form Person. In *Soziologische Aufklärung. Bd. 6. Die Soziologie und der Mensch* (3rd ed., pp. 137–148). VS Verlag für Sozialwissenschaften.

Luhmann, N. (2009). Interaktion, Organisation, Gesellschaft. In N. Luhmann (Ed.), *Soziologische Aufklärung. Bd. 3. Aufsätze zur Theorie der Gesellschaft* (6th ed., pp. 9–24). VS Verlag für Sozialwissenschaften.

Luhmann, N. (2012). *Macht* (4th ed.). UVK.

Luhmann, N. (2013). *Introduction to systems theory.* Polity Press.

Maes, J., & Schmitt, M. (2004). Gerechtigkeit und Gerechtigkeitspsychologie. In G. Sommer & A. Fuchs (Eds.), *Krieg und Frieden. Handbuch der Konflikt- und Friedenspsychologie* (pp. 182–194). Beltz PVU.

Marks, S. (2013). Scham – grundlegende Überlegungen. *Familiendynamik, 38*(2), 152–160.

Mattes, P. & Musfeld, T. (Eds.) (2005). *Psychologische Konstruktionen. Diskurse, Narrationen, Performanz.* Vandenhoeck & Ruprecht.
Maturana, H. R. & Varela, F. J. (1987). *The tree of knowledge: The biological roots of human understanding.* New Science Library/Shambhala Publications.
Mayer, B. (2000). *The dynamics of conflict resolution. A practitioner's guide.* Jossey-Bass.
McCann, C. (2020). *Apeirogon.* Random House. German version: (2021). *Apeirogon.* Rowohlt.
Mead, G. H. (1973). *Geist, Identität und Gesellschaft (Original 1934).* Suhrkamp.
Meuwly, N., Wilhelm, P., Eicher, V., & Perrez, M. (2011). Welchen Einfluss hat die Aufteilung von Hausarbeit und Kinderbetreuung auf Partnerschaftskonflikte und Partnerschaftszufriedenheit bei berufstätigen Paaren? *Zeitschrift für Familienforschung, 23*(1), 37–56.
Mikula, G. & Wenzel, M. (2000). Justice and social conflict. *International Journal of Psychology, 35*(2), 126–135.
Mintzberg, H. (2017). Developing theory about the development of theory. In S. W. Floyd & B. Woolridge (Eds.), *Handbook of middle management strategy process research* (pp. 177–196). Edward Elgar Publishing.
Montada, L. (2000). Gerechtigkeit und Rechtsgefühl in der Mediation. In A. Dieter, L. Montada, & A. Schulze (Eds.), *Gerechtigkeit im Konfliktmanagement und in der Mediation* (pp. 37–62). Campus.
Montada, L. (2003). Justice, equity, and fairness in human relations. In Th. J. Millon & M. Lerner (Eds.), *Handbook of Psychology, Vol. 5* (pp. 537–568). Wiley-Blackwell.
Montada, L. (2014). Gerechtigkeit – ein Kernproblem in Konflikten. *Konfliktdynamik, 3*(1), 26–34.
Moore, C. W. (2003). *The mediation process. Practical strategies for resolving conflict.* (3rd ed.). Jossey Bass.
Mote, J. E. (2001). From Schütz to Goffman: The search for social order. *The Review of Austrian Economics, 14*(2–3), 219–231.
Nagel, L. (2021). *Kybernetik, Kommunikation und Konflikt: Gregory Bateson und (s)eine kybernetische Konflikttheorie.* Carl Auer Systeme.
Nassehi, A. (2012). Paradoxie. In O. Jahraus, A. Nassehi, & et al. (Eds.), *Luhmann Handbuch. Leben, Werk, Wirkung* (pp. 110–111). J. B. Metzler.
Nassehi, A. (2017). *Die letzte Stunde der Wahrheit. Kritik der komplexitätsvergessenen Vernunft.* Murmann.
Nickerson, R. S. (1998). Confirmation bias: A ubiquitous phenomenon in many guises. *Review of General Psychology, 2*(2), 175–220. https://doi.org/10.1037/1089-2680.2.2.175
Olthof, J. (2017). *Handbook of narrative psychotherapy for children, adults, and families. Theory and practice.* Karnac.
Omer, H., Alon, N., & Schlippe, A. von (2007). Feindbilder. Psychologie der Dämonisierung. Vandenhoeck & Ruprecht.
Omer, H., Schlippe, A. von (2010). *Stärke statt Macht. Neue Autorität in Familie, Schule und Gemeinde.* Göttingen: Vandenhoeck & Ruprecht.
Omer, H., & Schlippe, A. von (2023). *Autorität durch Beziehung. Gewaltloser Widerstand in Beratung, Therapie, Erziehung und Gemeinde (10th revised ed.).* Vandenhoeck & Ruprecht.
Ortmann, G. (2003). *Regel und Ausnahme. Paradoxien sozialer Ordnung.* Suhrkamp.
Ortmann, G. (2011). *Kunst des Entscheidens.* Velbrück.
Papoušek, H., & Papoušek, M. (2002). Intuitive parenting. *Handbook of parenting. Volume 2: biology and ecology of parenting.* Lawrence Erlbaum.
Pfab, W. (2020). *Konfliktkommunikation am Arbeitsplatz. Grundlagen und Anregungen zur Konfliktbewältigung.* Springer.
Plate, M. (2013). *Grundlagen der Kommunikation.* Vandenhoeck & Ruprecht.
Plogstedt, S. (2008). *Abenteuer Erben. 25 Familienkonflikte.* Reclam.
Polkinghorne, D. E. (1988). *Narrative knowing and the human sciences.* State University of New York Press.

Ponschab, R. (2014). Die Erde ist eine Scheibe und andere Wahrheiten. *Zeitschrift für Konfliktmanagement, 17*(4), 125–128.
Ponschab, R. (2015). Mediation nach dem Harvard-Verhandlungs-Konzept. *Konfliktdynamik, 4*(4), 264–273. https://doi.org/10.5771/2193-0147-2015-4-264
Ponschab, R. (2018). Was macht man gegen Macht? *Konfliktdynamik, 7*(4), 256–263. https://doi.org/10.21706/kd-7-4-256
Pörksen, B. (2015). *Schlüsselwerke des Konstruktivismus* (2nd ed.). Springer VS.
Pörksen, B. (2019). Wahrheit und Skandal. *Konfliktdynamik, 8*(1), 12–15. https://doi.org/10.5771/2193-0147-2019-1-12
Pruitt, D. G., & Kim, S. H. (2004). *Social conflict: Escalation, stalemate, and settlement* (3rd. ed.). Mcgraw-Hill.
Raisch, M. (2022). *Emotionen in der systemischen Therapie.* Vandenhoeck & Ruprecht.
Ramsbotham, O., Miall, H., & Woodhouse, T. (2011). *Contemporary conflict resolution.* Polity Press.
Redlich, A. & Rogmann, J. J. (2014). Konfliktmoderation mit Gruppen. *Gruppendynamik und Organisationsberatung, 45*(2), 151–173.
Riedl, R. (1981). Die Folgen des Ursachendenkens. In P. Watzlawick (Ed.), *Die erfundene Wirklichkeit* (pp. 67–90). Piper.
Rispens, S. (2014). Beneficial and detrimental effects of conflict. In O. B. Ayoko, N. M. Ashkanasy, K. A. Jehn (Eds.), *Handbook of conflict management research* (pp. 19–32). Edward Elgar Publishing.
Rizzolatti, G. & Craighero, L. (2004). The mirror-neuron system. *Annual Review of Neuroscience, 27,* 169–192.
Robinson, S. L. & Rousseau, D. M. (1994). Violating the psychological contract: Not the exception but the norm. *Journal of Organizational Behavior, 15,* 249–259.
Roehling, M. (1997). The origins and early development of the psychological contract construct. *Journal of Management History, 3*(2), 204–217. https://doi.org/10.1108/13552529710171993
Rogers, C. (2012). *Client Centered Therapy (New Ed).* Hachette UK.
Rosenberg, M. (2015). *Nonviolent communication: A language of life* (3rd ed.). PuddleDancer Press.
Rost, W. (1990). *Emotionen. Elixiere des Lebens.* Springer.
Rotthaus, W. (2010). *Wozu erziehen? Entwurf einer systemischen Erziehung.* Carl Auer Systeme.
Rousseau, D. M. (1995). *Psychological Contracts in Organizations: Understanding written and unwritten agreements.* SAGE Publications.
Sandel, M. (2009). *Gerechtigkeit. Wie wir das Richtige tun.* Ullstein.
Satir, V. (1988). *The new peoplemaking.* Science and Behavior Books.
Schlippe, A. von (2014a). *Bevor das Kind in den Brunnen fällt! Konfliktmanagement als Kernaufgabe in Familienunternehmen (educational film).* Concadora.
Schlippe, A. von (2014b). Das Auftragskarussell – Ein Instrument der Klärung eigener Erwartungserwartungen. In T. Levold & M. Wirsching (Eds.), *Systemische Therapie und Beratung – das große Lehrbuch* (pp. 223–227). Carl Auer Systeme.
Schlippe, A. von (2014c). *Das kommt in den besten Familien vor. Systemische Konfliktberatung in Familien und Familienunternehmen.* Concadora.
Schlippe, A. von (2014d). Vertrauen. *Familienunternehmen und Strategie, 4*(3), 199–201.
Schlippe, A. von (2018a). Ein Businessplan für das Juwel: "Schräge kommunikative Anschlüsse". *Familiendynamik, 43*(3), 248–251.
Schlippe, A. von (2018b). Übung zur Musterunterbrechung bei Konflikten: Kleine Kreditangebote. *Systhema, 32*(1), 67–68.
Schlippe, A. von (2019a). Die Selbstorganisation eskalierender Konflikte – Reiseberichte aus Dämonistan. In C. Fischer (Ed.), *Kommunikation im Konflikt* (pp. 43–59). Beck.
Schlippe, A. von (2019b). Skizze einer Systemtheorie der Neuen Autorität – Was können wir von Unternehmerfamilien lernen? In B. Körner, M. Lemme, S. Ofner, T. von der Recke, C. See-

feldt, H. Thelen (Eds.), *Neue Autorität. Das Handbuch. Konzeptionelle Grundlagen, aktuelle Arbeitsfelder und neue Anwendungsgebiete* (pp. 86–102). Vandenhoeck & Ruprecht.

Schlippe, A. von (2020). Über die Verwandlung der Empörung. *Familiendynamik, 45*(1), 87.

Schlippe, A. von (2022a). Das Testament schafft Fakten. Erben, Vererbung und Gerechtigkeit. *Familiendynamik, 47*(1), 4–11.

Schlippe, A. von (2022b). Erzählen schafft Erinnerung. Die Verkörperung und transgenerationale Bedeutung von Geschichten in Familien. In P. Jakob, M. Borcsa, J. Olthof, A. von Schlippe (Eds.), *Narrative Praxis. Ein Handbuch für Beratung, Therapie und Coaching* (pp. 120–134). Vandenhoeck & Ruprecht.

Schlippe, A. von (2022c). Family businesses in coaching: Specific dynamics. In S. Greif, H. Möller, W. Scholl, J. Passmore, F. Müller (Eds.), *International Handbook of Evidence-based Coaching* (p. 325–336). Springer.

Schlippe, A. von & Frank, H. (2017). Conflict in family business in the light of systems theory. In F. Kellermanns, F. Hoy (Eds.), *The Routledge Companion to Family Business* (pp. 367–384). Routledge.

Schlippe, A. von & Groth, T. (2023). Company, family, business family: Systems-theoretical perspectives on the extension of three-circle thinking. In H. Kleve, T. Köllner (Eds.), *Sociology of the Business Family. Foundations, Recent Developments, and Future Perspectives* (pp. 259–303). Springer.

Schlippe, A. von & Hülsbeck, M. (2016). Psychologische Kontrakte in Familienunternehmen. *Familienunternehmen und Strategie, 4*, 122–127.

Schlippe, A. von & Jansen, T. (2020). Das Erwartungskarussell als Instrument zur Klärung komplexer Situationen im Coaching – vorgestellt am Beispiel der Nachfolge in Familienunternehmen. *Konfliktdynamik, 9*(2), 128–134. https://doi.org/10.5771/2193-0147-2020-2-128

Schlippe, A. von & Kummer, F. von (2021). Stichwort Konfliktpsychologie: Der fundamentale und der feindselige Attributionsfehler. *Familienunternehmen und Strategie, 11*(5), 202–203.

Schlippe, A. von & Quistorp, S. (2020). Der Preis der Gerechtigkeit. Ein Dilemma in Unternehmerfamilien. *Kontext, 51*(3), 281–289.

Schlippe, A. von & Rüsen, T. (2024). *Conflicts and conflict dynamics in business families Dealing with internal family disputes.* Springer. (in press)

Schlippe, A. von, Rüsen, T., & Groth, T. (2021). *The two sides of the business family. Governance and strategy across generations.* Berlin/New York: Springer

Schlippe, A. von & Schweitzer, J. (2012). *Lehrbuch der systemischen Therapie und Beratung I: Die Grundlagen.* Vandenhoeck & Ruprecht.

Schlippe, A. von & Schweitzer, J. (2015). *Systemic interventions.* Vandenhoeck & Ruprecht.

Schlippe, A. von & Schweitzer, J. (2019). *Gewusst wie – gewusst warum. Die Logik systemischer Interventionen.* Vandenhoeck & Ruprecht.

Schulz von Thun, F. (1981). *Miteinander Reden 1: Störungen und Klärungen.* Rowohlt.

Schulz von Thun, F. (2014). *Miteinander reden 3: Das "Innere Team" und situationsgerechte Kommunikation.* Rowohlt.

Schützeichel, R. (2004). *Soziologische Kommunikationstheorien.* UVK.

Selvini-Palazzoli, M., Boscolo, L., Cecchin, G., & Prata, G. (1977). *Paradoxon und Gegenparadoxon.* Klett-Cotta Verlag.

Shapiro, D. (2017). *Negotiating the nonnegotiable. How to resolve your most emotionally charged conflicts.* Penguin

Shapiro, D. & Burris, E. (2014). The role of voice in managing conflict. In O. B. Ayoko, N. M. Ashkanasy, & K. A. Jehn (Eds.), *Handbook of conflict management research* (pp. 173–192). Edward Elgar Publishing.

Sharp, G. (1960). *Gandhi wields the weapon of moral power.* Navajian.

Siegrist, J. (2000). Place, social exchange and health: proposed sociological framework. *Social Science & Medicine, 51*(9), 1283–1293.

Simon, F. B. (2001). *Tödliche Konflikte. Zur Selbstorganisation privater und öffentlicher Kriege*. Carl Auer Systeme.
Simon, F. B. (2004). Zur Systemtheorie der Emotionen. *Soziale Systeme, 10*(1), 111–139.
Simon, F. B. (2012). *Einführung in die Systemtheorie des Konflikts* (2nd ed.). Carl Auer Systeme.
Spencer Brown, G. (1994). *Laws of form*. Cognizer.
Sprenger, R. (2012). *Radikal führen*. Campus.
Stern, D. (2011). *Ausdrucksformen der Vitalität. Die Erforschung dynamischen Erlebens in der Psychotherapie, Entwicklungspsychologie und den Künsten*. Brandes & Apsel.
Stern, D. (2016). *Diary of a baby: What your child sees, feels, and experiences*. Basic Books.
Stern, D. (2020). *The motherhood constellation: A unified view of parent-infant psychotherapy*. Routledge.
Stierlin, H. (1979). Status der Gegenseitigkeit: die fünfte Perspektive des Heidelberger familiendynamischen Konzepts. *Familiendynamik, 4*(2), 106–116.
Stierlin, H. (2005). *Gerechtigkeit in nahen Beziehungen*. Carl Auer Systeme.
Straub, J. (Ed.). (2005). *Narration, identity, and historical consciousness* (Vol. 3). Berghahn Books.
Straub, J. (2010). Psychology, narrative and cultural memory, past and present. In A. Erll, A. Nünning (Eds.), *A companion to cultural memory studies* (pp. 215–228). De Gruyter.
Straub, J. (2019). *Das erzählte Selbst. Konturen einer interdisziplinären Theorie narrativer Identität*. Psychosozial.
Teubner, G., Lindahl, H., Christodoulidis, E., & Thornhill, Ch. (2011). Debate and dialogue: Constitutionalizing polycontexturality. *Social & Legal Studies, 20*(2) 209–252.
Then-Bergh, C. & Schlippe, A. von (2020). Neue Medien und die Eskalation von Konflikten. *Konfliktdynamik, 9*(4), 277–285.
Thiele, A. (2018). *Argumentieren unter Stress. Wie man unfaire Angriffe erfolgreich abwehrt* (18th ed.). dtv.
Thomas, W. I. & Thomas, D. S. (1928). *The child in America: Behavior problems and programs*. Knopf.
Tomasello, M. (2014). *Die Ursprünge der menschlichen Kommunikation* (3rd ed.), Suhrkamp. English version: 2008, *Origins of human communication*, MIT Press.
Tomasello, M. (2020). Mensch werden. Eine Theorie der Ontogenese. Suhrkamp. English version: 2019, *Becoming human: A theory of ontogeny*. Harvard University Press.
Tomasello, M. & Carpenter, M. (2007). Shared intentionality. *Developmental science, 10*(1), 121–125.
Ury, W. (2000). *The third side: Why we fight and how we can stop*. Penguin Books.
Valsiner, J., Molenaar, P. C., Lyra, M. C., & Chaudhary, N. (Eds.) (2009). *Dynamic process methodology in the social and developmental sciences*. Springer.
van der Heyden, L., Blondel, C., Carloc, R. S. (2005). Fair Process. Striving for Justice in Family Business. In: *Family Business Review, 18*(1), S. 1–21.
Varela, F. (1981). Der kreative Zirkel. Skizzen zur Naturgeschichte der Rückbezüglichkeit. In P. Watzlawick (Ed.), *Die erfundene Wirklichkeit. Wie wissen wir, was wir zu wissen glauben?* (pp. 294–309). Piper.
Vogd, W. (2013). Polykontexturalität: Die Erforschung komplexer systemischer Zusammenhänge in Theorie und Praxis. *Familiendynamik, 38*(1), 32–41.
Vogd, W. (2015). In Geschichten gefangen – Therapie als Erzählung und die Befreiung vom sinnlosen Sinn. Reflexionen zum kulturpolitischen Dilemma therapeutischer Berufe. *Verhaltenstherapie & Psychosoziale Praxis, 47*(1), 63–76.
de Waal, F. B. M. (2017). *Der Affe in uns. Warum wir sind, wie wir sind*. (5th ed.). dtv.
Watzlawick, P. (1977). *Die Möglichkeit des Andersseins*. Huber.
Watzlawick, P., Beavin, J., & Jackson, D. (1967). *Pragmatics of human communication*. Norton.
Weick, K. E. & Sutcliffe, K. M. (2007). *Managing the unexpected. Resilient performance in an age of uncertainty (2nd ed.)*. Jossey-Bass.

Weinblatt, U. (2013). Die Regulierung des Schamgefühls bei intensiven Eltern-Kind-Konflikten: Praktiken des gewaltlosen Widerstands, die die Öffentlichkeit einbeziehen. *Familiendynamik, 38*(1), 62–71.

Weinblatt, U. (2016). *Die Nähe ist ganz nah! Scham und Verletzungen in Beziehungen überwinden.* Vandenhoeck & Ruprecht.

Weinblatt, U. (2018). *Shame regulation therapy for families: a systemic mirroring approach.* Springer.

Weizsäcker, C. F. von (1977). *Der Garten des Menschlichen.* Hanser.

Welzer, H. (2010). Communicative memory. In A. Erll, A. Nünning (Eds.), *A companion to cultural memory studies* (pp. 285–300). De Gruyter.

Wempe, C. (2022). Redet ihr noch oder habt ihr schon geerbt? Familienpsychologische Überlegungen zum Thema Erbe. *Familiendynamik, 47*(1), 12–21.

Wetzel, D. (2022). Kontexte des Familiengedächtnisses –Aspekte, Funktionen und Formen des Erinnerns und des Vergessens. In P. Jakob, M. Borcsa, J. Olthof, & A. von Schlippe (Eds.), *Narrative Praxis. Ein Handbuch für Beratung, Therapie und Coaching* (pp. 105–119). Vandenhoeck & Ruprecht.

Willemse, J., & von Ameln, F. (2018). Die Interpunktion von Interaktion und Kommunikation. In Willemse, J., & von Ameln, F. (Eds.), *Theorie und Praxis des systemischen Ansatzes: Die Systemtheorie Watzlawicks und Luhmanns verständlich erklärt* (pp. 115–128). Springer.

Willi, J. (1982). *Couples in collusion.* Jason Aronson.

Wink, W. (2014). *Verwandlung der Mächte: Eine Theologie der Gewaltfreiheit.* Pustet.

Wittgenstein, L. (1968). *Tractatus logico-philosophicus* (5th ed.). Suhrkamp.

Wittgenstein, L. (2015). *Bemerkungen über die Grundlagen der Mathematik (Werkausgabe Band 6).* Suhrkamp.

Wright, L. (2016). *Dreizehn Tage im September: Das diplomatische Meisterstück von Camp David.* Theiss. English version: 2014, *Thirteen days in September.* Random House.

Zhao, H., Wayne, S., Glibkowski, B., & Bravo, J. (2007). The impact of psychological contract breach on work-related outcomes: A meta-analysis. *Personnel Psychology, 60,* 647–680.

Zellweger, Th. (2017). *Managing the family business. Theory and practice.* Cheltenham/UK, Northampton, MA/USA: Edward Elgar Publishing.